ALCAEUS
by Hubert Martin, Jr.

:ERIES

ıre

ity

nology

The island of Lesbos contributed two great names to the history of Greek lyric poetry, those of Sappho and her contemporary and countryman Alcaeus. Hubert Martin, Jr. presents a study of Alcaeus' poetry that is thorough, comprehensive, and firmly anchored to the Greek texts that have actually survived. The study is designed for both classicists and the reading public.

Deeply implicated in the political turmoil that shook his city-state Mytilene in the late seventh and early sixth centuries B.C., Alcaeus is introduced to the reader as a poet frequently motivated by political involvement and partisan emotion. His poetry is then analyzed for its images, themes, figures, content, and for the literary influences which worked upon it and which it in turn generated. Treated prominently in this analysis are Alcaeus' drinking songs, nautical allegories, and Hymns; his poetic reaction to the Homeric epic; his thematic debts to Hesiod and Archilochus; his literary relationship with Sappho; and his inspiration of Horace. Finally, the metrical structure of Alcaeus' poetry is subjected to explanation and illustration.

Alcaeus emerges from the author's interpretive crucible as a partisan poet who was at the same time a lyric craftsman of the highest order.

(TWAS 210)

TWAYNE'S WORLD AUTHORS SERIES (TWAS)

The purpose of TWAS is to survey the major writers —novelists, dramatists, historians, poets, philosophers, and critics—of the nations of the world. Among the national literatures covered are those of Australia, Canada, China, Eastern Europe, France, Germany, Greece, India, Italy, Japan, Latin America, the Netherlands, New Zealand, Poland, Russia, Scandinavia, Spain, and the African nations, as well as Hebrew, Yiddish, and Latin Classical literatures. This survey is complemented by Twayne's United States Authors Series and English Authors Series.

The intent of each volume in these series is to present a critical-analytical study of the works of the writer; to include biographical and historical material that may be necessary for understanding, appreciation, and critical appraisal of the writer; and to present all material in clear, concise English—but not to vitiate the scholarly content of the work by doing so.

Alcaeus

By HUBERT MARTIN, JR.

University of Kentucky

ABOUT THE AUTHOR

Born in 1932, Hubert Martin, Jr. attended
the University of Chattanooga as an under-
graduate and received a Ph.D. in Classics
from Johns Hopkins in 1958. He has taught
Classics at Randolph-Macon College and the
University of North Carolina, and is presently an associate professor of Classics at
the University of Kentucky. He has held a
fellowship at the Center for Hellenic Studies
and has published frequently in the *Ameri-
can Journal of Philology* and other classical
journals. In addition to Aeolic poetry, his
chief academic interests are his teaching and
the interpretation of Plutarch's *Lives* and
Moralia.

York

Printed in U.S.A. by
NOBLE OFFSET PRINTERS, INC.
New York, N.Y. 10003

Contents

Chronology

From Lullies: *Griechische Vasen der Reifarchaischen Zeit* (Munich, 1953), pl. 94.

Preface

This book is an attempt to present Alcaeus to the general reader and, at the same time, to furnish a study of his surviving poetry that will be of service to classicists as well. My goal has been to analyze this poetry comprehensively and thoroughly, but to presume on my reader's part no knowledge of the Greek language and only a rudimentary acquaintance with ancient Greek literature. Of the three parts to my book (The Poet as Partisan, The Poet as Poet, The Poet as Metrician) the general reader may prefer to stop short of the last, since it is intended largely for classicists and for those interested in metrics and poetic rhythm. Despite its technical nature, however, it is designed to be comprehensible to the Greekless reader and supposes no prior knowledge of Greek metrics.

My Greek text has consistently been that edited by Edgar Lobel and Denys Page, *Poetarum Lesbiorum Fragmenta* (Oxford, 1955); and I have striven to present no interpretation of Alcaeus's poetry that is inconsistent with this text. The fragments (no poem by Alcaeus has survived complete) are regularly cited by the combination letter-number designation they have in Lobel and Page's edition (for example, A 6 or Z 2), but I have usually added to this designation a title of my own invention. Unless otherwise indicated, all translations of Alcaeus are also my own. Among modern studies, I have benefited most from Denys Page's *Sappho and Alcaeus* (Oxford, 1955).

My debts are numerous. To the University of Kentucky for a Summer Research Fellowship and for a Faculty Research Grant. To my wife Diana and to my colleagues John Scarborough, Katharine H. Shaw, Louis Swift, and Edgar Warren, all of whom read and criticized substantial portions of my manuscript.

HUBERT MARTIN, JR.

Lexington, Kentucky

PART I

The Poet as Partisan

CHAPTER 1

The Historical Milieu

ALCAEUS was born in the city-state of Mytilene on the Aegean island of Lesbos, in the midst of an era aptly designated by A. R. Burn as "The Lyric Age of Greece."[1] The exact date of his birth is uncertain. It must have been around 630 B.C. or during the following decade. As to the date of his death, the most precise statement possible is that it was probably no earlier than 580 B.C. Our knowledge of his purely domestic life is confined to two items: he had at least two brothers, and his family belonged to Mytilene's aristocratic elite. No mention of a wife or children has been preserved. Much, however, is known about Alcaeus's public life, which profoundly and pervasively affected the content of his poetry and which will be discussed presently. Alcaeus's high station in Mytilenean society, though nowhere explicitly claimed by him, is nevertheless abundantly demonstrated by his own vigorous political activity, by the prominence and aristocratic credentials of his political enemies, and, above all else, by his reference to possessions and privileges enjoyed by "my father and my father's father" ("Exile" = G 2, lines 20-21). The combination of ancestral prerogative and political prestige is a sure sign of noble lineage during the era in which Alcaeus lived and wrote.

As a poet, Alcaeus was "lyric" (*lyrikos*) in the true and literal sense of the word; that is, his poetry was composed to be sung and the singing was to be accompanied by the lyre.[2] Most, if not all, of his poems may be classified as "monodic," in the sense that they were to be sung by a single person furnishing his own musical accompaniment. Presumably, it was originally Alcaeus himself who both sang and played the lyre. There is insufficient evidence to decide whether any of his Hymns were intended for choral presentation.

Time has dealt harshly with Alcaeus's compositions, for not a single complete poem has survived to the present. During subsequent antiquity, however, while copies of his verses were still

15

in relatively common circulation, he was frequently quoted for a variety of literary, philological, and metrical reasons by writers whose works (including, of course, these quotations) have been preserved; and, during the twentieth century, the sands of Oxyrhynchus in Egypt have yielded numerous fragments of poems in the form of mutilated papyrus copies.[3] From this union of fragment and quotation a corpus of Alcaeus's poetry has been assembled in modern times that enables us to evaluate him from both a linguistic and a literary-critical perspective, to describe the meters in which he composed, and to make general observations about the nature and content of his poetry.

The independent, short poem was Alcaeus's chosen mode of expression, and the surviving pieces indicate a typical length of anywhere between eight and forty verses to the poem. (He must have written some longer compositions; how much longer we cannot say.) Some of the poems are in the form of convivial songs; others, of Hymns to deities or of narrations of myth and legend. Many include precise references and symbolic allusions, all in an intensely partisan tone, to contemporary Mytilenean politics and political figures. There are descriptions of nature, nautical allegories, exhortations to drinking, and accounts of personal frustration and disappointment. Due to the absence of whole poems, the brevity of the quotations, and the mutilated condition of the papyrus fragments, it is easier for the critic to speak comprehensively of themes, motifs, references, allusions, and images than it is for him to outline the full content of individual poems or to trace patterns of thought and mood throughout a given poem.

The focus of Part I of this book will be on the political and historical references and allusions in Alcaeus's poetry, the content of which is thoroughly conditioned by its author's partisan involvement in the political affairs of Mytilene throughout his active lifetime. Indeed, the content of many a poem has been wrought out of the political circumstances serving as its backdrop. To a remarkable degree it is impossible to separate Alcaeus the partisan from Alcaeus the poet, and the separation attempted in this book will be more a matter of emphasis than of essence. Any critical dissection of the political and historical base of Alcaeus's poetry, however, is in need of an introductory sketch of certain events that are beyond the confines of Alcaeus's chronological, political, and poetic vision.

Lesbos is a large island of 665 square miles situated off the northwest coast of Asia Minor, within easy sailing distance of the Hellespont and fabled Troy. Greek settlers first arrived there from the Balkan peninsula during the early Dark Age (probably before the end of the second millennium B.C.), thereby initiating a migration pattern that was to last for several centuries.[4] The dialect of the Greek language spoken by these settlers was Aeolic, and the lands they occupied on and off the coast of Asia Minor became known as Aeolis. The Aeolians soon extended their colonizing efforts beyond Lesbos to the adjacent mainland and gradually spread their settlements, in varying degrees of concentration, along the coast of Asia Minor over an area terminated by the Gulf of Smyrna on the south and reaching far enough north to include the plain of Troy. The colonization of the southern part of this littoral area may have begun as early as 1000 B.C., and before the end of the eighth century the Troad had become Aeolic territory.

In historical times, political affairs on Lesbos came to be dominated by five, independent city-states: Mytilene on the eastern coast, Methymna and Antissa in the north, Eresos in the west, and Pyrrha on the central gulf. Of these, Alcaeus's native city Mytilene was the largest and most powerful, having gained control of the entire eastern part of the island and having overseas interests as far away as Naucratis in Egypt. Though independent, the cities of Lesbos participated in some sort of religious alliance—the Greek word for it is *amphictyony*—which probably had political connotations: Alcaeus speaks of a common sanctuary founded by the men of Lesbos, in which they set up altars in honor of the blessed immortals ("The Prayer" = G 1, lines 1-4).

Long before Alcaeus's birth in the last third of the seventh century, his city-state Mytilene had completed the transition, standard throughout the Greek world, from monarchy to aristocratic government. Its ruling class consisted of aristocratic clans, such as the Archeanactids ("Sons-of-the-ruling-lord") and the Penthilids, the latter tracing their origins through Penthilus, son of Orestes, to the very conqueror of Troy. Alcaeus, writing from exile, expressed his yearning "to hear the Assembly [*agora*] and the Council [*bolla*] being summoned by the heralds" ("Exile" = G 2, lines 18-20). The Assembly was the more general and democratic of the two bodies, and we can be sure it was in the smaller Council that whatever clique of aristocrats were in power at a given moment exercised their control over the political life of Mytilene. What we do not know is precisely how a man qualified for membership in the Assembly or gained a seat on the Council. Alcaeus twice mentions the people of Mytilene (*damos*). In "Pittacus" (D 12) the *damos* is unfavorably portrayed as responsible for civil strife and for the success of the tyrant Pittacus (lines 10-13), and in "The Prayer" (G 1) Alcaeus tells of an oath he took, along with a group of partisans, either to save the *damos* from its troubles or to die in the attempt (lines 14-20). Again, it is unknown how effective a voice this nebulous *damos* had in the Assembly, or whether it had to express its political will primarily through extraconstitutional means.

In the course of the century extending roughly from 650 to 550 B.C., the city-state of Mytilene saw the birth, rise to prominence, and death of three figures who were to become her most illustrious offspring and who left a permanent and distinctive mark on Greek letters and Greek political history: the lyric poets Alcaeus and Sappho and the tyrant-sage Pittacus. The literary flourishing of this island polis was thus accompanied by political turmoil of the gravest sort, and whether through allusion or direct reference, the personal and literary effect of this turmoil flashes brilliantly throughout Alcaeus's surviving verses. The nautical allegories, especially "The Ship: I" (A 6) and "The Ship: II" (Z 2), which symbolize the political fortunes of Alcaeus's party, are sufficient to illustrate the point.[5] One might also cite the famous exhortation in which Alcaeus proclaims the death of a political enemy, who had established himself as tyrant of Mytilene and driven Alcaeus and his party into exile: "Now's the time to get drunk and with some vigor/ to drink, for Myrsilus has died, indeed he has . . . " ("Myrsilus Is Dead!" = Z 8).

For more than a century before Alcaeus's birth, the Greek world had been undergoing a rapid, inexorable process of colonial, industrial, and commercial expansion—a process that was, in polis after polis, to culminate in political upheaval and social change. In Mytilene the culmination took place during Alcaeus's lifetime and dictated the political milieu in which he moved and wrote. At the very beginning of the period in question (about 750 B.C. or slightly later), Greece in the geographical sense consisted only of central and southern mainland Greece,

the Aegean coast of Asia Minor, and the intervening islands
(including Rhodes and Crete). The entire northern coast of the
Aegean was still *barbaria*. Politically, in the nascent city-states
aristocratic clans had already stripped the kings of their powers,
or were in steady process of diluting these powers and ar-
rogating to themselves the political, military, and judicial
prerogatives formerly enjoyed by the reigning monarchs. Militar-
ily, the safety of the polis depended heavily on cavalry, which
was provided by the aristocrats, who alone among the inhabitants
were capable of outfitting themselves with armor and horse.
Political authority and military importance thus went hand in
hand. Land was the basis and primary form of wealth, and
the landed aristocrats carried out their business and commercial
transactions without benefit of coinage.[6]

By the time of Alcaeus's death in the first half of the sixth
century, or shortly thereafter, say by 550 B.C., all this had changed
drastically. Greek colonies, many of them destined to surpass
their founding cities in size, prestige, and even power, had been
firmly and abundantly established throughout the Mediterranean
basin, from the most distant shores of the Black Sea in the east
to the littoral of France and Spain in the far west. The eastern
two thirds of Sicily had become a Greek island; and the southern
part of the Italian peninsula, its coast rimmed with Greek
colonies, was known as Great Greece (*hē megalē Hellas*).
Though much of the northern coast of Africa was Phoenician
domain, the Greek colony of Cyrene far eastward of the
Phoenician settlements prospered; and Naucratis became a flourishing Greek emporium at the western mouth of the Nile.
Alcaeus's Mytilene, though not a great colonizing polis, was
commercially active during the Age of Colonization and participated in the economic growth that was one of its salient features:
archaeological evidence indicates Mytilene enjoyed prestigious
economic ties throughout the northeastern Aegean area;[7] and
along with Ionians of Chios, Teos, Phocaea, and Clazomenae
and with Dorians of Rhodes, Cnidus, Halicarnassus, and Phaselis,
Mytilenean colonists founded the great Hellenion at Naucratis
and supervised the commercial life of this port city.[8] Indeed,
Sappho's brother Charaxus was an active businessman, for we
are reliably informed of one occasion on which he transported
Lesbian wine to Naucratis for sale—and found the leisure and the

resources to purchase, at a great price, the freedom of the famous
Naucratite courtesan Rhodopis.[9]

The change, however, was not defined exclusively by the
external feature of colonial expansion and commercial activity:
political reverberations shook the city-states of the motherland.
By the time of Alcaeus's death the once all-powerful aristocracies
had in their turn been smashed or were in disarray. Often, as
at Argos, Corinth, Sicyon, Athens, Samos, Ephesus, Miletus,
and at Mytilene, the agent of their political demise was a
tyrannos (the English translation "tyrant" is not quite accurate),
an autocrat who exercised and maintained his authority outside
any constitutional framework. The aristocrats had supported and
fostered colonization, at least some of them had augmented
their resources through commercial activity, but they proved
generally inept at relaxing the political, social, and economic
tensions resulting from the Age of Colonization.

Industry, commerce, and the widespread introduction of
coinage made it possible for nonaristocrats to accumulate wealth
and acquire fiscal prestige. Military tactics changed: cavalry
ceased to be basic to the welfare of the polis, and in its place
stood the hoplite phalanx, a force of heavy-armed infantry whose
ranks were full of men of the new middle class, nonaristocrats
to be sure and prospered without benefit of noble ancestry by
the economic circumstances just outlined, but because of their
recently gained wealth able to furnish their own armor and
weapons—and, therefore, essential to the defense of the state.
Wealth and military importance thus devolved on a group still
lacking in political privilege. The aristocratic clans refused to
open their ranks or share their prerogatives, and a wellspring of
revolution came into being. Another such wellspring was a
peasant class that was impoverished as well as unprivileged,
farmers heavily in debt to rich landowners, some of them already
reduced to semiserfdom and standing to profit by a redistribution
of land.[10] Alcaeus, partisan aristocrat and reactionary that he is,
nevertheless seems at least vaguely aware that the world is not
what it once was, that social and economic changes have taken
place. He implicitly acknowledges, although in cynical tones,
the existence—and the potential for social and political prominence—of the new middle class when he agrees with Aristodemus
that "money's the man, and no poor man is any good or held in
honor" ("A Saying of Aristodemus" = Z 37); and an impoverished

and discontented lower class hovers somewhere in the background behind another fragment ("Poverty and Helplessness" =
Z 41): "A harsh, relentless ill is Poverty [*Penia*], and she a great/
people [*laos*] conquers in alliance with her sister Helplessness
[*Amachania*]."

At Mytilene and elsewhere, social and political chaos was
arrested by the advent of *tyrannoi*, often aristocrats themselves,
who renounced the concept of political privilege advocated by
their birth-conscious fellow nobles and molded a following out
of their polis' unprivileged groups.[11] *Tyrannos* is not a technical
term. As commonly used in antiquity and by modern interpreters
of Greek constitutional history, it designates an autocrat who
seizes and maintains power in a state by extraconstitutional and
extralegal means. (The "constitutional tyrannies" of Solon at
Athens and Pittacus at Mytilene, whose autocratic positions,
while more or less absolute when assumed, were legally sanc-
tioned and chronologically limited, are to be classified as variations of a common political theme.) In many city-states tyranny
was the only alternative to wholesale revolution and chaos, and
it generally served as a transition from rule by politically effete
aristocracies to more broadly based and constitutionally viable
forms of government, such as Athenian democracy after Solon
and the Pisistratids or Mytilenean oligarchy after Pittacus.
The general course of tyranny at Mytilene will provide a framework, both chronological and factual, within which to examine
in the next chapter Alcaeus's poetic reaction to the political
events in which he was so deeply involved.

Although firm dates are not available for the events about to
be narrated and related to Alcaeus's poetry, it is possible to set
up a chronological framework based on the life and career of
Pittacus. The dates constituting this framework may be accepted
as establishing a reliable relative chronology and as roughly
accurate in an absolute sense.[12] Pittacus was born several years
before 640 B.C., participated in overthrowing the tyrant
Melanchrus sometime between 612 and 609 B.C., and distinguished himself in battle around Sigeum between 609 and
600 B.C. After ruling Mytilene from about 590 to 580 B.C., he lived
on in retirement for another decade until his death circa 570 B.C.
During Pittacus's lifetime Mytilene experienced a succession of
three tyrannies together with a war with Athens for possession
of Sigeum in the Troad; and Alcaeus himself spent much time

in exile, both on Lesbos beyond the borders of Mytilene and
across the sea, perhaps in Egypt. The first tyrant, Melanchrus,
was eliminated by an alliance involving Pittacus with the
brothers of Alcaeus; and the second, Myrsilus, was at one time
(whether before or after he seized power is uncertain) opposed
by a similar faction, including Pittacus again and, this time,
Alcaeus himself. Pittacus, however, deserted the alliance to
combine with Myrsilus, and after the latter's death was in turn
chosen *tyrannos* by a willing citizenry. It is significant that
Pittacus did not seize the tyranny with the aid of an armed
bodyguard but that, instead, it was conferred on him by some
sort of an elective process. Our ancient sources list two factors
as motivating the Mytileneans: Pittacus's conduct of the war
against Athens and fear of an exiled faction led by Antimenidas
and his brother Alcaeus.[13] Tradition has it that Pittacus captured
Alcaeus and then pardoned him.[14]

CHAPTER 2

Politics and Poetry

"NOW'S the time to get drunk and with some vigor/ to drink, for Myrsilus has died, indeed he has . . ." ("Myrsilus Is Dead!" = Z 8). Partisan hatred is for Alcaeus a basic and continuing source of poetic inspiration. It often emerges, as here in these verses announcing the death of a hated political enemy, in brazen, overt invective. Elsewhere, as in the nautical allegories, it is sublimated into vivid, precisely drawn symbols. Always, if Alcaeus's extant verse is a reliable criterion, its subjection to the technical refinements of meter and diction was smooth and unobtrusive. Its expression in Alcaeus's references and allusions to the times and persons of Melanchrus, Myrsilus, and Pittacus will be our present concern.

I Melanchrus

The tyrant Melanchrus is as shadowy a historical personage as Alcaeus's relationship with him is unclear. We are reliably informed by Strabo (XIII, 2, 3) that he was the object of Alcaeus's poetic invective and by Diogenes Laertius (I, 74) that he was overthrown by a coalition led by Pittacus and including the brothers of Alcaeus. Yet in the single verse constituting Z 7 Alcaeus *seems* to be praising him: "Melanchrus worthy of respect into the city. . . ." The verse is quoted by our source exclusively for metrical reasons and, therefore, without regard for either sense or context; though a complete line of poetry, it lacks even a verb and is syntactically no more than a series of phrases. If the full sentence were preserved from which this verse has been excerpted we would probably discover that Alcaeus is describing Melanchrus as someone who "seemed" or "pretended to be worthy of respect" and who disappointed expectations. There is no need to suspect the information provided by Strabo of being either incomplete or inaccurate. Diogenes's omission of Alcaeus's name from the coalition that

23

overthrew Melanchrus is perhaps to be accounted for by
"Memories" (D 17), a mutilated, thirteen-line papyrus fragment
offering the following words and phrases (I translate the entire
fragment to give the reader an idea of the type of material
Alcaeus's interpreters must frequently work with. Dots indicate
a lacuna in the text):

<pre>
        . . . .
        . . . .
        . . . previously shown
        . . . those failing disgrace
    5   . . . necessity
        . . . I remember; for still a boy
        . . . who was small I was sitting on.
        . . . I know . . .
        . . . [a reference to the Penthilids] . . .
   10   . . . and now he overthrew
        . . . [a reference to someone "base-born"]
        . . . [a reference to tyranny]
        . . . .
</pre>

Lines 6-7 indicate that Alcaeus is narrating an event that
occurred when he was still a small boy—and, thus, too young to
participate. Lines 9-12 *seem* to describe the career of Pittacus; for
we know that he married into the Penthilid clan,[1] that he overthrew Melanchrus,[2] and that he became tyrant of Mytilene.
Also, Alcaeus elsewhere characterizes Pittacus as "base-born"
(Z 24). In "Memories" (D 17), therefore, Alcaeus *may* be telling
of the overthrow of Melanchrus and *may* be indicating that this
event occurred before he himself was old enough to take part in
public afairs. Contextual analysis of Z 7 and "Memories" is of
necessity steeped in speculation. What is not speculative is
Alcaeus's partisan spirit, which flashes brightly even from such
meager fragments.

II   *Myrsilus*

The career of Myrsilus has left its mark on Alcaeus as both
partisan and poet, on the latter in the form of a distinctive thread
of influence that is traceable throughout the Alcaean corpus. We
are, however, often unable to describe the purely literary aspects
of this influence, even when it is certainly there, since our
knowledge of many a reference to Myrsilus is derived from a

scholiast or commentator whose remark is as ill-preserved as the poem which he is explaining; or else the name Myrsilus glares at us in isolation, devoid of context and destitute of even its full complement of letters.

In the case of two, and probably three, poems (E 1, M 8 [a], and R 1), a scholion does no more than reveal that Myrsilus was the subject of a reference;[3] and it is likely that... *silon*... is to be filled out to ... *Myrsilon* [accusative case]... at K 38, line 2. Scholia to the paltry remains of D 2 and E 3, however, are more informative.[4] E 3 must have contained a reference (whether extended or in the form of an allusion it is impossible to say) to the tyranny of Myrsilus, for the scholiast comments that during their first exile Alcaeus and his faction plotted unsuccessfully against Myrsilus and had to seek refuge at Pyrrha. And it may be inferred from the fragmentary scholion to D 2 (a) that in this poem Alcaeus addressed to his friend Bycchis an account of the plot against Myrsilus and of its abortive fruition: an attempt was made on Myrsilus's life somewhere between Pyrrha and Mytilene, but the tyrant was saved by his bodyguards (*dory- phoroi*). Finally, a recently published papyrus fragment of a commentary to Alcaeus (number 2733 in the Oxyrhynchus collection) offers a series of references to "the son of Cleanor" (line 11), "Myrsilus" (line 12), and exile (line 14).[5] The son of Cleanor is not otherwise known, and the papyrus is too ill-preserved to permit anything more than speculation as to the relation among these three references.

Valuable historical information is furnished, either directly or indirectly, by two poems. From the commentary listed as V 1, column i in Lobel and Page's edition we learn that Myrsilus himself apparently endured exile at one time in his career; for the commentator describes at lines 15-21 a poem addressed by Alcaeus to one Mnemon, in which the latter is excused for assisting Myrsilus in his return (*kathodos*) by furnishing him a boat.[6] In addition, from "Pittacus" (D 12) we learn that Myrsilus was once in some unspecified way associated with Pittacus in power, as is disclosed by Alcaeus's cynical comment on Pittacus as tyrant: "Let him devour the city even as he did with Myrsilus" (line 7). It is likely, though not certain, that "The Prayer" (G 1) contained a reference to this same alliance, for a thoroughgoing castigation of Pittacus for treachery and lawlessness (lines 13-25) is soon followed at line 28 by a verse from which the word "Myrsilus," but nothing else, has survived.

The two-verse quotation at the beginning of this chapter, which is all that remains of "Myrsilus Is Dead!" (Z 8), is Alcaeus's most famous overt reference to Myrsilus—or, for that matter, to any contemporary political figure. In addition, the political behavior of Myrsilus helped motivate Alcaeus in the creation of his best-known and most influential image, the storm-racked ship in the nautical allegories of "The Ship: I" (A 6) and "The Ship: II" (Z 2). In demonstrating this fact and explaining its nature it will be necessary to anticipate some of the arguments and conclusions presented in Chapter 4, which contains detailed analysis of all poems that are either surely or possibly allegorical. I will, however, confine my present attention to the two poems just mentioned, for these are the only ones that certainly involve the tyranny of Myrsilus and are fully germane to my immediate critical interests.

We may begin by examining the more legible portions of the two poems in question, both composed in Alcaics and both opening with a description of a ship foundering in a storm. For "The Ship: II" (Z 2), I will use Richmond Lattimore's verse translation, which is a stress imitation of the original metrical scheme. "The Ship: I" (A 6) will be offered as translated into English prose by Denys Page, whose rendering is both accurate and reasonable in its use of conjectural translations, which will be enclosed in square brackets.[7] Again, a lacuna in the Greek text will be indicated by dots.

The Ship: II (Z 2)

> I cannot understand how the winds are set
> against each other. Now from this side and now
>   from that the waves roll. We between them
>   run with the wind in our black ship driven,
>
> hard pressed and laboring under the giant storm.
> All round the mast-step washes the sea we shipped.
>   You can see through the sail already
>   where there are opening rents within it.
>
> The forestays slacken. . . .

The Ship: I (A 6)

This wave again comes [like?] the one before:

it will give us much labor to bale out, when it
enters the vessel's . . .

. . . let us fortify the . . . with all speed,
and run into a secure harbor.

And let not unmanly hesitance take hold of any
one [of us]: a great . . . is clear before us.
Remember our [toils] of yesterday: now let
each prove himself a steadfast man.

And let us not disgrace [by cowardice] our
noble fathers lying under the earth . . .

The image of "The Ship: II" is vividly and precisely drawn, and there is within the extent portion of this poem no internal evidence of either allegory or political allusion. The same may be said of "The Ship: I," though less emphatically, since the exhortations of its third and fourth stanzas seem more appropriate to preparation for battle than to behavior during a storm at sea. Nevertheless, the case for an allegorical interpretation of these two images would be somewhat weak, were it not for the explanatory comments of Heraclitus, an obscure though perceptive critic who wrote, perhaps during the first century of our era, a work cited variously as *Allegories* or *Homeric Questions.*[8] The first nine verses of "The Ship: II" (Z 2)—that is, all of the verses whose translation is given above—are quoted by Heraclitus in illustration of his claim that Alcaeus frequently composed allegories in which the disturbance produced by political tyranny is symbolized by stormy weather at sea. Heraclitus goes on to amplify this allegorical explanation by indicating that in the quoted verses Alcaeus is alluding to the tyrannical conspiracy of Myrsilus against the Mytileneans; and Heraclitus immediately cites the first three verses of "The Ship: I" as another example of an enigmatic allusion to the times of Myrsilus. This second quotation is followed by the criticism that Alcaeus's allegories contain an excessive amount of sea imagery, since he likens most of the evils caused by tyrants to storms at sea. Heraclitus's references to the disturbance produced by political tyranny and to the evils caused by tyrants indicate that he has been fully taken in by Alcaeus's partisan assessment of Myrsilus's career and tyranny. They also indicate that Heraclitus

is following Alcaeus's thought closely; and, since Heraclitus
had before him full poems, as against the parts and fragments of
poems with which Alcaeus's modern critics are confronted, there
is every reason to trust his allegorical exegesis of these two
nautical images.

Heraclitus is commenting on a general characteristic of
Alcaeus's poetry and is using the two Myrsilus-oriented allegories
chiefly for illustrations; and, as a result, his comments are themselves too general to allow us to determine the exact point
Myrsilus had reached in his career toward the tyranny when
the poems under scrutiny were composed. Indeed, the composition dates may have differed considerably; and Heraclitus's
comments, imprecise as they are on this point, might incline us
to conclude that "The Ship: II" (Z 2) was actually written first,
before Myrsilus had seized the tyranny, while "The Ship: I"
(A 6) symbolizes with its storm his behavior and the conditions
in Mytilene after he had fully gratified his political ambitions
and established himself as tyrant. Or again, Alcaeus may have
given in neither poem information sufficient to allow Heraclitus,
or anyone else, to determine with full certainty whether its storm
represented a situation before or after Myrsilus had seized
absolute power. And from a purely aesthetic point of view, it
would make little difference to Alcaeus as a poet whether the bad
conditions symbolized by his allegorical storm were generated by
an established or by a prospective tyrant.

Myrsilus thus furnished Alcaeus a goodly portion of the
historical raw material out of which he fashioned his best-known
nautical allegories. The other portion was furnished by the
political and military reaction of Alcaeus's faction to the career
and successes of Myrsilus. The argumentation of Chapter 4,
as applied to the allegories of "The Ship I" (A 6) and "The Ship:
II" (Z 2), may be anticipatively summarized as follows. In
addition to the storm, which represents the political evils
generated by the tyrant Myrsilus, each allegory contains two
fundamental symbols, the ship (together with its crew) and the
voyage which the ship is making. The former represents Alcaeus's
"party"—"faction" would be a blunter and perhaps more accurate
designation, though we can be sure that Alcaeus would see it as a
party motivated by honorable concern for the welfare of his
polis—the latter, the course of action being taken by this party
in its struggle against Myrsilus. The course of action symbolized

by the voyage of "The Ship: II" may be quite general; that of "The Ship: I" is perhaps a definite military enterprise, as is indicated by the exhortations of its third and fourth stanzas, especially by "let us not disgrace [by cowardice] our noble fathers lying under the earth."

III *Pittacus*

The type of absolute authority (*monarchia*) conferred on Pittacus by the Mytileneans is defined by Aristotle as an "elective tyranny" (*hairetē tyrannis*); and Pittacus himself is classified as an *aisymnētēs* ("overseer"), who was elected to this position for the express purpose of protecting the state against an exiled faction led by Alcaeus and his brother Antimenidas.[9] Diogenes Laertius indicates that Pittacus had earned the confidence of his countrymen through his conduct, as general, of the war against Athens over Sigeum, during which he slew the Athenian commander Phrynon, an Olympic victor, in single combat (*monomachia*).[10] Also, his basis of power must have been considerably strengthened by the marriage into the Penthilid clan that is scornfully remarked by Alcaeus in "Pittacus" (D 12, line 6): "And now that he has married into the House of Atreus . . . / let him devour the city. . . "[11] The basic accuracy of Aristotle's analysis and classification of Pittacus's position is confirmed by Alcaeus himself, when in "The People's Choice" (Z 24) he acknowledges that, in effect, the Mytileneans "elected" Pittacus *tyrannos*: "the base-born/ Pittacus over that docile and ill-starred city/ did they in mobs establish as tyrant, amidst shouts of praise." The polis is "ill-starred" (*barydaimōn*); and the same ugly truth of Pittacus elected *tyrannos* is again admitted, less bluntly to be sure but in the same fatalistic tones, in the last stanza of "Pittacus" (D 12), where Alcaeus pleads for an end to civil strife, "which some Olympian/ aroused, leading the people into folly/ and to Pittacus giving glory fair" (lines 11-13).

A moderate reformer who instigated legislation but left the constitution intact, Pittacus used his absolute authority to break the power of the aristocratic clans, and then gave his polis back its independence.[12] His law to curb drunkenness became famous (offenses committed in a state of intoxication received double penalties); and he himself acquired a reputation for wisdom and clemency, a reputation which was secured for posterity by his inclusion among the Seven Sages. (Ancient writers also assigned the Athenian Solon and the natural philosopher Thales to this group.) Despite these illustrious historical and traditional credentials, Pittacus is the consistent target of Alcaeus's most vitriolic poetic invective.[13] His physical appearance was demeaned in poems no longer extant by such ignominious epithets as "Flat-foot," "Acne-foot," "Prancer," and "Fats" (Z 106), as also at verse 21 of "The Prayer" (G 1) by "Pot-belly"; and he is once, probably three times, designated as "base-born" (*kakopatridas*: "The People's Choice" [Z 24]; "Memories" [D 17], line 12; and D 48).[14] Perhaps in his depiction of Pittacus Alcaeus was partially inspired by the Homeric description of Thersites, whose offensive physical appearance functions as a complement to the baseness of his social position and demagogic politics (*Iliad* II, lines 216-19):

This was the ugliest man who came beneath Ilion. He was / bandy-legged and went lame on one foot, with shoulders / stooped and drawn together over his chest, and above this / his skull went up to a point with the wool grown up sparsely upon it.[15]

Pittacus is twice metaphorically depicted as a ravening beast devouring its prey—the prey being his own polis Mytilene: "Let him devour the city even as he did with Myrsilus" ("Pittacus" = D 12, line 7), and "indifferently with his paws/ he trampled on his oaths and now devours/ the city . . ." ("The Prayer" = G 1, lines 22-24).[16] Pittacus's offensive appearance and allegedly ignoble lineage are thus matched by baseness of character; and, if the surviving fragments are a reliable guide, the theme of Pittacus the oath-breaker was frequently and brazenly intoned by Alcaeus throughout his politically motivated verse. Its fullest extant expression is in "The Prayer" (G 1). The verses from this poem quoted above are introduced, first, by a curse on Pittacus ("Let an avenging Fury go after the Son of Hyrrhas," lines 13-14) and, then, by a justification of the curse (lines 14-24): though Pittacus had taken an oath of loyalty to his comrades, when they swore either to save the people from their troubles or to lay down their lives in the attempt, "indifferently . . ./ he trampled on his oaths." The quality of the papyrus text deteriorates rapidly after the middle of verse 24, but the surviving phrases of the next stanza (lines 25-28) indicate a complaint about an illegal agreement between Pittacus and Myrsilus. This same violation of oaths by Pittacus probably accounts for the phrase "in violation of oaths" in the first preserved verse of H 28; for, though this poem is pervasively mutilated from beginning to end, it appears to be describing Pittacus's political career. And lines 9-12 of the fragmentary commentary listed as X (9) in Lobel and Page's edition give sure proof of still another poem in which Alcaeus chastised Pittacus as a breaker of oaths and betrayer of comrades.

An assortment of scholia and comments, together with isolated bits and pieces of poems far more distinctive for what has perished than for what survives, reveals that Alcaeus composed numerous other poems (in addition to those cited above) in which Pittacus was the subject of either reference or allusion. Indeed, he was probably the primary subject of some of these poems. The evidence for a reference to Pittacus in H 31, column ii is sure but circumscribed: it is confined to the *phitt* . . . of line 4. This is obviously the beginning of the Aeolic form of Pittacus's name and may be at least partially restored to *Phittak-*, but its inflection must remain a mystery. Other references or allusions to Pittacus are attested by marginal scholia to E 1 (at line 24) and to H 18, though in each instance both scholion and verse commented on are mutilated beyond repair, and by the phrase "about Pittacus" in a commentary (V 1, line 24) on a lost poem of political complexion. The poem itself, as we can tell from the commentary, was addressed to a man named Mnemon, who had at one time given assistance to Myrsilus; it is, however, unclear how the reference or allusion to Pittacus was worked into the poem. Two additional poems, moreover, attacked Pittacus directly. One, H 2, from which only two legible verses have survived, was obviously composed before Pittacus became *tyrannos;* for it offered a warning: "This man who seeks supreme authority/ will soon subvert our city. . . . " A scribe has written in "Pittacus" above "this man." The other, the poem being commented on in the first eight lines of X (9), was written after Pittacus had received the tyranny, since it contained, we are informed by the commentator, a reference to Pittacus and a metaphorical allusion to stopping "the *tyrannos* from his wicked insolence." The isolated words "Pittacus" (line 2) and "Alcaeus" (line 4), which have survived from another commentary dealing with Alcaeus (fragment 77 of papyrus number 2506 in the Oxyrhynchus collection),[17] merely serve to corroborate what is by now well established; namely, that in his own peculiar way Pittacus was for Alcaeus a constant source of poetic inspiration.

IV *More Stasiotica*

In antiquity all the poems so far discussed in this chapter (that is, all of the politically motivated poems, which amount to a goodly portion of the entire extant corpus) were classified together under the adjectival rubric *stasiotic* ("factional," "partisan"). Strabo (XIII, 2, 3) explains that these stasiotic poems dealt with political discord at Mytilene during the period of the tyrants and that in them Alcaeus attacked, among others, Pittacus, Myrsilus, Melanchrus, and the Cleanactids. (The only surviving reference in Alcaeus's verse to the Cleanactids is at E 1, line 23, in a mutilated but illustrious context including also references to Myrsilus, Pittacus, and one of the Archeanactids.) Strabo, almost as an afterthought, raises the suspicion that Alcaeus himself may have had personal designs on the tyranny of Mytilene. The excessive vehemence of Alcaeus's abuse of Myrsilus and Pittacus supports this suspicion and, in turn, raises questions about his patriotism and the genuineness of his concern for the *damos* of Mytilene. Was he committed to a preservation of the old order and sincerely convinced of its political efficacy? Or was he at heart a revolutionary who opposed tyranny only when it was in the possession of a political enemy? Or, again, did he covet the tyranny simply as a means of revitalizing the past and eliminating all progressive opposition?

Whatever the answer to these and similar questions, the story of Alcaeus's stasiotic verse is not yet complete; for there are a number of poems, in addition to those already examined, that must obviously be classified as stasiotic, though they cannot be certainly connected with a particular tyrant. Of this class are "The Reef" (D 15), "Foresight" (L 1), and "The Vineyard" (F 5), allegorical poems which will be described and analyzed in Chapter 4, as well as "The Smoldering Log" (D 16). The remains of this last poem are meager; however, by supplementing its surviving words and phrases with information afforded in scholia to verses 4 and 6, it is possible to arrive at a reasonably full knowledge of its content. The poem bluntly chastises the Mytileneans for not resisting a prospective tyrant (lines 2-5), who is then metaphorically compared to a smoldering log that has not yet burst into flames (lines 6-7); and Alcaeus desperately urges his countrymen to extinguish the log before the fire becomes unmanageable. There is, however, no indication as to whether the log symbolizes Melanchrus, Myrsilus, or Pittacus.

Four other stasiotic poems *may* have focused their invective on Pittacus. As was previously remarked in this chapter, because of references to the Penthilids, to overthrowing [Melanchrus?], to someone "base-born," and to tyranny, it seems likely, though not certain, that verses 9-12 of the highly fragmentary "Memories" (D 17) are describing the career of Pittacus, since he married into the Penthilid clan, overthrew Melanchrus, is called "base-born" in Z 24, and, of course, eventually became *tyrannos* of Mytilene. A similar degree of hesitation is appropriate to taking Pittacus as the subject of H 28, a fragment even more mutilated than "Memories." There are, however, in H 28 two phrases suggestive of Pittacus: "in violation of oaths" (line 1) and "against Phrynon" (line 17). It will be recalled that Pittacus's violation of his oaths is the main theme of "The Prayer" (G 1) and of the poem being commented on at lines 9-12 of X (9), and that Pittacus's conquest of the Athenian commander Phrynon in single combat at Sigeum was a major item among his political credentials. It has been commonly assumed that the man depicted as an incult carouser in verses 3-10 of "New Man" (D 14) is Pittacus's father and that Pittacus himself is the person addressed in the next three verses: "And you, sir, born of such [a mother? a family?], have you/ the same renown as free-born men/ who come from noble parents...?"[18] It is true that these last three verses are reminiscent of Pittacus's Alcaean epithet "base-born" and that the Thracian origins of Pittacus's father would encourage a depiction such as that of the man being abused in the preceding verses.[19] It is also true that there is nowhere an express identification of either person, and that Alcaeus must have had many political enemies whom he could accuse of bad manners or low birth. "New Man" (D 14) is surely an exercise in political invective. The object of its insults may or may not be Pittacus. And a similar appraisal is appropriate to A 5, one of whose fragmented stanzas (lines 11-14) contains the word *basileus*, which frequently means "king," as well as references to a marriage and to a bodyguard of lance-bearers. A personal bodyguard is characteristic of a *tyrannos;* the contextually associated marriage suggests Pittacus.[20]

Vocabulary and references suggestive of or appropriate to stasiotic poems are exhibited by many meager fragments, often too meager to permit definitive classification and never sufficient for anything more than speculative analysis. In D 9, for example, references in successive verses (3-4) to the altar of Apollo and to preventing "anyone of those base-born" from doing something indicate a stasiotic poem, in which Alcaeus perhaps spoke with pride of hereditary priesthoods reserved for those nobly born and to be denied to a more democratic opposition. Again, when in the single verse listed as Z 26 Alcaeus says "I am horribly miserable" and then mentions "my friends," one suspects that these are friends in the political rather than the absolute sense of the word. Too, a stasiotic background seems probable for the poem in which Alcaeus defended himself against the charge, brought by one Amardis, of being responsible for the death of a certain man (a "friend"?) whose name has been lost. (Our knowledge of this poem and of its general content is derived from a commentary published subsequently to Lobel and Page's *Poetarum Lesbiorum Fragmenta*.)[21] And it is likely that the misfortunes twice mentioned in the first three verses of "The Plea" (B 18) are also political, perhaps even military, instead of personal: "Over my head (for I have suffered much) pour myrrh/ and over my hoary chest.../ Let them drink, evils...." It must be admitted, however, that the lacunae, indicated by the series of dots, leave open other possibilities. This is emphatically true of those innumerable references to self that are scattered in fragmentary isolation throughout the Alcaean corpus. A few examples will suffice: "for I do not have" ("The Harlot" = F 3 [b], line 22), "tell me" (F 8, line 6), "I" (A 11, line 4 and B 5, line 4), "and me" (F 13, line 4), and "hanging [in uncertainty?] for us" (item 315 in Lobel-Page).

As the champion of a political order that had fully demonstrated its weaknesses and was experiencing a rapid demise during the period of the tyrants, Alcaeus was rather consistently the spokesman of a losing cause. The successful coup that removed Melanchrus from the tyranny only served to create a power vacuum that was soon filled by Myrsilus and that gave Pittacus an opportunity to move into a position only one step removed from absolute authority. Indeed, his base of support augmented by military prestige and a judicious marriage, Pittacus was catapulted into the tyranny by a threat to orderly government posed by Alcaeus's own party. Pittacus's moderate and successful tyranny and his clemency toward Alcaeus, if this latter tradition is accurate, must have been a bitter draught for a man of Alcaeus's aristocratic convictions and partisan mettle.[22] Bitter draughts, however, had long been steady fare for Alcaeus and his comrades, if we are to judge from the resignation and pessimism of "The Ship: I" (A 6), "The Ship: II" (Z 2), "Pittacus" (D 12), and "The Prayer" (G 1), as well as from the evidence that Alcaeus spent a goodly portion of his public career in exile and in open rebellion against whatever passed for established authority at Mytilene. We have already remarked the threat (and it must have been a military threat) that accounted for Pittacus's being appointed *tyrannos;* the fact that "The Ship: I" (A 6) alludes to some military campaign; and, in connection with E 3 and D 2 (a), the abortive plot and the period of exile at Pyrrha during Myrsilus's tyranny. Too, "The Prayer" (G 1), since it is addressed to deities whose sanctuary was pan-Lesbian and, therefore, at some distance from the actual city of Mytilene, must have been uttered, at least dramatically, during a period of exile.

It is also impossible to relate to a specific *tyrannos* many other remarks by Alcaeus about exile and about military and political enterprises. This is the case with the reference to the gods' giving "us victory" (item 314 in Lobel-Page), to Zeus's fulfilling "our purpose" (Z 38), and to the "task" (*ergon*, line 8) for which the military equipment described in "The Armory" (Z 34) is intended. It is equally uncertain under which *tyrannos* Alcaeus experienced the misfortunes being related in "Exile" (G 2): "a wretched life I/ live, enduring a rugged existence,/ longing to hear the Assembly/ and ... the Council being summoned by the heralds" (lines 16-20) and "in exile far from home ... " (line 24). Also, Strabo's report (I, 37) that Alcaeus told of a journey to Egypt may well indicate a poem in which he described an exile abroad; and the slight fragments of H 9 suggest—but no more than suggest—an emphatic contrast between former prosperity and present misery in exile.

Four poems give evidence, in varying degrees of cogency, of mercenary service by Alcaeus and members of his faction, very likely during a period of exile when resources were failing. "The Sword" (Z 27) describes a magnificent sword with hilt of ivory and gold, which Alcaeus's brother Antimenidas brought back from the Near East, where he fought as ally to the Babylonians and distinguished himself by slaying a giant warrior. "Babylon and Ascalon" (B 16) is a curious fragment. The top, bottom, and entire left-hand portion of the papyrus on which it was copied have decayed; but the right-hand portion of the sixth through the nineteenth verses offers twenty-three complete words, many of them in the form of phrases. Mercenary service in the Near East by Alcaeus and his comrades is suggested by a succession of references to "the sea" (line 6), destroying (line 9), "holy Babylon" (line 10), "Ascalon" (line 11), military activity that seems to involve the storming of a citadel (lines 12-13), death (line 15), and to "crowns for us" (lines 17). Far scantier than the remnants of "Babylon and Ascalon" (B 16) are those of D 5; yet the verb "gave" (line 4) and a reference to "staters" in some multiple of a thousand (line 7) again suggest mercenary service, though with no indication as to where or for whom. Finally, the first stanza of "The Fox" (D 11) clearly states that the Lydians paid Alcaeus's party to perform a specific military task: "Father Zeus, the Lydians in anger/ at misfortunes two thousand staters/ to us gave, if haply we can into the holy [?]/ city force our way."[23] What is not clear is whether this payment was for mercenary service in the Near East, or represents Lydian intervention in the political affairs of Lesbos.

Two interpretative cruxes in the stanza quoted account for this absence of clarity. First, it is syntactically uncertain at whose misfortunes the Lydians are angry, their own or those of Alcaeus's faction;[24] and, secondly, the city in question, since its identity is unsure, may be either on the island of Lesbos or on the Asiatic mainland. If the Greek word at the end of verse 3 is correctly translated "holy," this city (*polis* is the word rendered as "city") may even be Mytilene. The word translated "holy," however, is only partially preserved; and there is the enticing possibility that it should be restored to the name of a small town on Lesbos, "Ira," instead of to an adjective meaning "holy." Whatever polis was to be seized, Alcaeus and his comrades were handsomely rewarded for their prospective services; for two thousand staters is enough to raise a small army, or to ransom a whole city.[25] How they fared in this enterprise is another matter, for a succeeding reference to someone who behaved "like a fox of crafty mind" (lines 6-8) raises the suspicion that something went wrong.

An ancient commentary published since the appearance of Lobel and Page's edition of the Sapphic and Alcaean corpus sums up, in a sense, both the character (though not the facts) of Alcaeus's political career and the condition of our primary evidence for it. The commentary is published as Oxyrhynchus Papyrus number 2506, and the pertinent sections are Fragments 98 and 102.[26] At lines 4-8 of Fragment 98 it is argued that a certain reference by Alcaeus to his brother proves that Antimenidas was still alive at the time of "the second exile and the action at the bridge." The commentator next (lines 8-11) indicates that neither did Alcaeus die "in this action"; but his remarks then disintegrate amid references to what appears to be a third exile and return (*kathodos*) and to a war, the latter in context with the names of two Asiatic monarchs, Astyages and Alyattes. Nothing else is known about this action at the bridge (presumably Alcaeus mentioned it in a poem), and it is only a possibility that the reference to the two monarchs indicates mercenary service in the Near East on the part of Alcaeus and his brother. It is likely, however, that such service by Antimenidas was the major theme of Fragment 102, in which the commentator refers successively to "the king of the Lydians" (lines 2-3), to "Antimenidas the brother of Alcaeus" (lines 5-6), and then to war and danger (line 9). The appearance of the names "Pittacus" and "Croesus" in the last two lines raises many questions, but answers none. What does clearly emerge from these two fragments is an impression of partisan activity and political failure.

The partisan hatred that Alcaeus distilled into unobtrusively polished verse may reasonably be attributed to aristocratic pride and political failure. The preceding pages have catalogued Alcaeus's fluent and vituperative expression of this hatred in his poetry and at the same time have surveyed the numerous references and allusions indicative of failure, hardship, and frustrated enterprises. Alcaeus the partisan is thus Alcaeus the poet. The converse of this equation, however, is only a partial truth; and in the succeeding chapters we will examine innumerable facets of Alcaeus's poetic genius that are either completely devoid of or only remotely related to partisan politics.

PART II

The Poet as Poet

CHAPTER 3

The Making of Images

"AND I think that to transfuse emotion—not to transmit thought but to set up in the reader's sense a vibration corresponding to what was felt by the writer—is the peculiar function of poetry." So A. E. Housman in "The Name and Nature of Poetry" summarizes his conception of poetry and of what separates poetry from nonpoetry.[1] In amplification of this summary Housman goes on to offer the corollaries that "poetry is not the thing said but a way of saying it" and "that the intellect is not the fount of poetry, that it may actually hinder production, and that it cannot even be trusted to recognize poetry when produced." This conception of the nature and function of poetry will be taken as a point of departure for the immediate analysis of Alcaeus as poet—as distinct from Alcaeus as *narrative* poet, or as *partisan* poet. The present chapter will attempt to isolate and to examine the poetic element within the poems of Alcaeus, that element which is apart from their intellectual content or subject matter and upon which their success or failure as poetry depends.

To express Housman's conception of poetry in other terms, we might say that the primary and fundamental appeal of poetry is to the feelings rather than the intellect and that this emotional appeal is quite apart from any intellectual appeal that the literary, moral, political, social, or theological ideas of a poem may present. This point may be illustrated by Milton's reference in *Paradise Lost* to Mulciber, who was

> thrown by angry Jove
> Sheer o'er the crystal battlements: from morn
> To noon he fell, from noon to dewey eve,
> A summer's day; and with the setting sun
> Dropped from the zenith like a falling star,
> On Lemnos the Aegean isle. . . .
> (Book I, lines 741-46)

This extended reference to Greek mythology has absolutely
nothing to do with the theological content of *Paradise Lost;*[2]
nor does it advance Milton's narrative, whose needs would have
been amply satisfied with the simple statement that Mulciber was
the architect of the "fabric huge" just described (lines 710-32).
In fact, the reference actually impedes the narrative, for Milton
immediately adds that the story was not true (lines 746-51).
And yet it is upon such verses as these that Milton's appeal and
success as a poet ultimately depends; and had he not been able
to interlace *Paradise Lost* with such verses of sheer poetry, the
poem might have stimulated theological analysis of an esoteric
variety; but it would never have been admired as poetry.

It is above all else through the agency of rhythm and imagery,
both of which appeal to the senses and feelings *before* they
stimulate intellectual analysis, that the poet is able "to transfuse
emotion" and to establish emotional rapport with his reader or
listener. If this be doubted, let us strip the Miltonic passage
just quoted of its rhythm and of as many of its images as possible
and see what the results are:

One morning during the summer Jove became angry at Mulciber
and threw him off Mt. Olympus. After falling all day long he landed
at sunset on Lemnos, an island in the Aegean Sea.

This is clear, narrative prose, and all the facts are present; yet
it is certainly not poetry. Along with their rhythm and images
Milton's verses have lost their emotional content and thereby
their power to transfuse emotion within the reader.

The rhythms of Greek poetry are in part beyond the grasp
of even the specialist because of our inability to reproduce with
full accuracy the language as it was spoken and sung in antiquity,
and what can be said about the rhythms employed by Alcaeus
will have to be said in the rather technical section on metrics,
which is placed at the end of this book. Yet it is possible to
isolate and describe Alcaeus's images and to examine his imaginal
vocabulary. Such will be the task of the present chapter. (*Image*
will be used in the broad sense of any description of or reference
to a concrete object, specific act, or sensory experience.)

One preliminary note should be mentioned about my critical
methodology. The treatment of Alcaeus's use of traditional,
especially epic, vocabulary and themes will be temporarily post-
poned; and in the immediate discussion of his imaging I will

avoid making a distinction between, on the one hand, images contrived by Alcaeus himself and, on the other, those inherent in the language and diction he is employing. For example, Alcaeus twice, once in "Castor and Polydeuces" (B 2 [a], line 12) and once in "The Ship: II" (Z 2, line 4), describes a ship as "dark," thus employing an epithet frequently used in the Homeric poems to describe the actual appearance of a ship;[3] and in "Achilles" (B 10, lines 9-10) he refers to the consummation of a marriage with an image common to Greek literature ("he loosed the maiden's girdle").[4] In such situations as these the image and accompanying vocabulary will at present be discussed as Alcaeus's own, though in fact they are inherent in the language and diction of Greek poetry. It is my belief that no matter whether Alcaeus creates his own image or borrows one that is traditional, the basic effect on the reader's sense is the same. Also, at this early period it is not always easy to determine whether images and vocabulary are original or traditional.

Let us first examine two general characteristics of poetic imaging, as they apply to Alcaeus. One is the tendency to refer to the specific and concrete rather than the general and abstract. The other is the use of descriptive epithets and phrases that focus the reader's attention on a clear and concrete feature of an object to which reference is made. It is not that these two categories are mutually exclusive. Indeed, there is much overlapping between them. For purposes of critical analysis, however, it will be convenient to treat them separately.

The former characteristic is especially apparent in Alcaeus's references to himself. In "Exile" (G 2, lines 16-20), for example, instead of saying abstractly "I yearn to return from exile," he tells the reader what he yearns to *hear* in his own country: "the Assembly and the Council being summoned by the heralds." Not only does the poet make the point that he longs to return home; he tries to make it emphatically and vividly by indicating precisely what passes through his mind when he thinks of home. Again, in "The Prayer" (G 1, lines 1-12) he depicts himself as actually standing in the sacred presence of Zeus, Dionysus, and Aeolia and pleading with these deities to answer his prayers and rescue his comrades and himself from hardship and exile. His feelings are not simply recounted; they are put in the more concrete form of a prayer spoken in the first person and are addressed directly to the deities before whose altars he stands.

And though the prayer opens with general pleading (lines 9-12), it soon turns to specific references to Alcaeus's hatred for Pittacus ("let an avenging Fury go after the son of Hyrrhas," lines 13-14) and to the fact that Pittacus betrayed his comrades and trampled on his oaths (lines 14-24). And in "The Plea" (B 18, lines 1-2) he could have said "I am an old man who has suffered much, so comfort me." Instead he chose clear and vivid imagery to express these feelings: "Over my head (for I have suffered much) pour myrrh/ and over my hoary chest. . . . " The abstract thought "I am an old man" is expressed in the form of a concrete reference to his "hoary chest," and the plea for comfort as a plea for a specific act of comfort.

The same predilection for the specific and concrete is apparent in Alcaeus's references to Pittacus, his erstwhile ally become enemy, whom he characterized as a faithless turncoat and betrayer of comrades in "The Prayer" (G 1, lines 14-24). Though Alcaeus's differences with Pittacus were political, social, and, perhaps, personal, his verbal attacks on the tyrant frequently focused on purely physical features that had nothing to do with either his personal character or his political abilities. In "The Prayer" (G 1, line 21), he is contemptuously designated "Potbelly," and we learn from Z 106 that Alcaeus also assigned him the sobriquets "Flat-foot," "Acne-foot," "Prancer,"[5] and "Fats." Thus the reader's attention is directed not toward abstract qualities but toward concrete features that can actually be seen. And Alcaeus eschews the general in favor of the specific in "The Sword" (Z 27), when in what amounts to a metrical tour de force he gives the exact height of a giant warrior slain by his brother (lines 5-7): he was only one hand's breadth short of being five royal cubits tall.

The specific and the concrete are also prominent in Alcaeus's passing references to conditions and events. In "The Fox" (D 11) Alcaeus indicates that he and his comrades were hired by Lydians for precisely "two thousand staters" (lines 2-3; he does *not* say simply for "a huge sum of money"). And in "Let Us Drink" (Z 22) the command "mix the wine" (line 4) is accompanied by precise instructions that it is to be a strong drink containing only one part of water to two parts wine.[6] Moreover, to be alive is "to behold the clear light of the sun" ("Sisyphus" = B 6 A, lines 3-4), and to die is figuratively either to cross "swirling Acheron" ("Sisyphus" = B 6 A, lines 2-3 and 8) or to enter "the house of Hades" (B 16, line 15). Too, it may be that the enigmatically preserved reference to someone's beard being black at F 6, line 9 is an image indicating that someone was in the prime of life. Other examples are afforded by "Helen" (N 1, lines 15-16), where the general thought that there was much destruction on the plains of Troy is conveyed by a specific reference to many chariots lying in the dust. By D 13, a two-line fragment in which the idea to invite to a lavish feast is expressed as "to invite for kid and pork."[7] By "Let Us Drink" (Z 22), where the opening exhortation, "Let us drink," is repeated more concretely four lines later as "let cup strike against cup," a forceful image with connotations of conviviality and heavy drinking. By "New Man" (D 14, line 10) with "the bottom of the jar kept clinking" (since it was struck by the serving ladle when the wine ran low)[8] used in place of "large quantities of wine were consumed." And finally and most picturesquely by "Achilles" (B 10, lines 9-10), where the poet indicates that Peleus and Thetis consummated their marriage with "he loosed the maiden's girdle," a compact image not only stressing the innocence of the bride but also vividly depicting the respective roles of male and female from both a physical and an emotional perspective.

We may properly conclude this consideration of the first of the two general characteristics of Alcaeus's imagining—that is, his interest in the specific and concrete—by examining several of his more comprehensive descriptions. Despite the mutilated condition of the latter part of "The Ship: II" (Z 2 + K 5 [a] ii), the preserved verses indicate exactly what is happening to the ship as it is wrecked by a storm (lines 6-9): the bilge is rising above the masthold, the sail is full of great rents, the *agkyrrai* (whatever part of the rigging is designated by this precise and rather technical word)[9] are weakening. And in "The Armory" (Z 34) Alcaeus offers concise yet detailed descriptions of many of the catalogued items: "shining helmets from which white horse-hair plumes nod down" (lines 3-4), "shining bronze greaves which conceal the pegs on which they hang" (lines 4-5), "cuirasses of new linen and hollow shields scattered about, and beside them sword blades from Chalcis . . ." (lines 6-7). Again, one can almost feel the heat and ennui of the Aeolic summer as Alcaeus lists its specific and concrete features ("Summer" = Z 23): the dogstar in the heavens, all creation thirsty from the heat, the shrill chirping of the cicada, the artichoke in bloom, lean men, and women on the make.

I do not mean to imply by the preceding discussion that Alcaeus's poetry is an uninterrupted series of images and specific references. In fact, in "Summer" (Z 23), the poem just mentioned, immediately after the reference to the dogstar there is a brief general statement that the season is harsh (line 2), which of itself is so vague that it could describe winter as well as summer. At the same time, the general statement is so brief as to be absorbed by the surrounding images and from them to take on connotations of heat and ennui. A similar relation between abstract and concrete seems to have existed in "Winter" (Z 14, lines 1-4), where the somewhat general reference to "a great storm out of heaven" (lines 1-2) is followed by an image of frozen streams (line 2). (I say "seems," since the bulk of lines 3-4 are missing, and we can only infer from "Summer" [Z 23] that they contained winter images.)

Several other examples of Alcaeus's use of general and abstract diction are worth noting. In "The Fox" (D 11) an abstract "misfortunes" and a concrete "two thousand staters" are juxtaposed, the two phrases constituting the entire second line of the poem: "Father Zeus, the Lydians distressed at/ misfortunes two thousand staters/ to us gave. . . ." And the vague and abstract language of the final stanza of "Pittacus" (D 12) is broken only by the imaginal epithet "spirit-gnawing" and an explicit reference to the subject of the poem: "Let us cease from spirit-gnawing strife/ and fighting with kin, which some Olympian/ aroused, leading the people into folly/ and to Pittacus giving glory fair." Finally, two generally descriptive phrases are skillfully inserted in "The Armory" (Z 34) to punctuate the precise descriptions of the various items of military gear that are hanging about and strewn on the floor. The "white horse-hair plumes" that nod down from shining helmets (lines 3-4) are vaguely designated as "adornments for the heads of men" (line 4); and the "shining, bronze greaves which conceal the pegs on which they hang" (lines 4-5) become even more vaguely "a defense against a powerful missile" (line 5). Not only do these general phrases lend variety to the passage; with their epic connotations they raise it above the ordinary and give it a certain grandeur that would otherwise be lacking.[10]

Let us now turn to the second of the two general features of

Alcaeus's imaging—the use of descriptive epithets and phrases that focus the reader's attention on a clear and concrete feature of an object to which reference is made. Frequently the modifier has no direct bearing on the literal sense of a passage and is employed solely for its imaginal effect. This is particularly true in the case of natural objects. Heaven is "snowy" (Z 32) (as anyone knows who has observed it on a bright, white-cloud day), frost "icey" (O 1, line 3), and earth either "dark" ("Sisyphus" = B 6 A, line 10; "Exile" = G 2, line 29) or "broad" ("Castor and Polydeuces" = B 2, line 5). The sea is designated variously as "hoary" (Z 36; "The Harlot" = F 3 [b], line 27; V 1, lines 10-11), "briny" (Z 10), "surging" ("The Hebrus" = B 13, line 2), and "wine-dark" ("Ajax and Cassandra" = Q 1, line 25).[11] With similar variety, the Acheron is "swirling" ("Sisyphus" = B 6 A, lines 2 and 8); the personified Cephissus "great" and "surging" (A I [c], near end); while the waters of the personified Castalia are described as "silver" (A I [c], near end) and those of a mountain stream simply as "cold" ("Birds" = F 1, line 8). In this last mentioned poem, the adjectives "fragrant," "gleaming," "vineyard-rich," and "greenish" are used in the description of a natural scene (lines 6 ff.), but the fragmentary state of the poem makes it impossible to know what noun any of them modifies.

Epithets and adjectives are similarly applied to gods, men, and animals; and again the modifier is frequently without direct bearing on context, being chosen exclusively for its imaginal powers. Zeus is "aegis-bearing" (Z 19), Iris "wearing fair slippers" ("Hymn to Eros" = Z 3, line 2), and Zephyr "golden-haired" ("Hymn to Eros" = Z 3, line 3). In the case of groups, dead men are described as "clad in earth" ("The Prayer" = G 1, line 17), warriors as "quick-eyed" ("Helen" = N 1, line 16), Lesbian maidens participating in a beauty contest as "with flowing robes" ("Exile" = G 2, line 33), and horses as either "bay" ("Achilles" = B 10, line 14) or "swift-footed" ("Castor and Polydeuces" = B 2 [a], line 6). Also, the reader's attention is drawn to the "thighs" (which noun was probably accompanied by an epithet, though the mutilated state of the papyrus rules out certainty on this score) and "soft hands" of maidens bathing in the Hebrus ("The Hebrus" = B 13, lines 5-7), and wild ducks are assigned the epithets "with motley necks" and "with long wings" ("Wild Ducks" = Z 21, line 2).

Because of the highly fragmentary state in which Alcaeus's

poems have survived, critical judgments as to the relation of a given modifier to the over-all context and imagery of a poem are at best hazardous. Nevertheless, I am inclined to view all of the modifiers cited in the two preceding paragraphs as fundamentally ornamental—that is, as employed chiefly for cosmetic purposes and as having little or no direct bearing on the intellectual content and literal meaning of the poem. This is, however, not true of the adjective "hoary" in line 2 of "The Plea" (B 18), for we have seen that in this poem Alcaeus expresses the abstract thought "I am an old man" in the form of an image, a reference to his "hoary chest." It may well be that there was also a specific and immediate appropriateness in the references to the dark eyes and dark hair of Lycus (Z 107) and in the adjectives applied to Sappho in the one surviving line of the poem addressed to her (Z 61): "violet-tressed, holy, gentle-smiling Sappho."

It should be stressed, however, that even ornamental modifiers may have an immediate poetic appropriateness insofar as they contribute to the atmosphere or mood the poet is striving to create. This is certainly true of many of the ornamental modifiers mentioned above. And this truth may be further illustrated by examining the modifiers applied to man-made objects in two poems represented by remains sufficient to allow reasonably extensive analysis of their imagery. The modifiers of the items of military gear listed in "The Armory" (Z 34) all have a purely ornamental, imaginal function (*"shining* helmets from which *white horse-hair* plumes nod down," lines 3-4; *"shining, bronze* greaves," lines 4-5; "cuirasses *of new linen* and *hollow* shields," line 6); at the same time they contribute abundantly to the mood of optimism and the atmosphere of grand pageantry that the poem so effectively conveys. Again, in "The Sword" (Z 27), without the rich and vivid adjectives describing its hilt in lines 1-2 ("ivory," "overlaid with gold"), this sword would be an inadequate symbol of the "great feat" (line 4) performed by Alcaeus's brother. We may speculate that in the reference to "the helmet shot with gold," which is about all that remains of Z 5, the adjective served the total atmosphere of the poem as well as the specific image in which it was involved. If it is correct that the "honey-sweet" wine and wine "sharper than thistles" (Z 46) symbolize respectively good times and bad times, then it is reasonable to conclude that in "Winter" (Z 14) Alcaeus assigned the adjective "honied" to the wine which is ordered (lines 7-8) to enhance the atmosphere of good times and conviviality with which the poem exudes.

Other imaginal epithets attached to man-made objects, though they still draw the reader's attention to a specific feature of the object, nevertheless carry narrower or more conventional connotations. Ships are either "dark" ("Castor and Polydeuces" = B 2 [a], line 12; "The Ship: II" = Z 2, line 4) or "well-benched" ("Castor and Polydeuces" = B 2 [a], line 9). Also, in "Dill and Myrrh" (Z 39) garlands are "plaited" and myrrh "sweet," the unidentifiable objects of Z 60 are "shining," and Helen and Menelaus's marriage bed is covered "with a fair spread" ("Helen" = N 1, line 8).

In conclusion, several general or abstract nouns are rendered more vivid by the application of imaginal modifiers. Spring is "flowery" (Z 44); the Assembly and the Council mentioned in "Exile" (G 2) "being summoned by the heralds" (lines 18-20); and death "'chilling" ("Castor and Polydeuces" = B 2 [a], lines 7-8; D 3, line 14),[12] which epithet should be taken to refer both literally to the effect of death on the corpse and figuratively to the thought of death on human beings.

CHAPTER 4

A Selection of Themes

FROM a thematic point of view, Alcaeus is most widely known as a creator of drinking songs and nautical allegories. Wine flashes as a leitmotif throughout his poetic remains, and two of his best-known poems ("The Ship: I" = A 6 and "The Ship: II" = Z 2) depict storm-racked ships which have traditionally been regarded as allegorical symbols. This is far from the whole story, for some of Alcaeus's finest verses have nothing to do with either wine or ships. Nevertheless, because of both their frequency and their renown it seems appropriate to immediately segregate these two subjects for special treatment. In the present chapter I will, first, trace the wine motif throughout the body of Alcaeus's poetry, and then examine in detail each of the nautical poems. In the process it will be critically expedient to associate the far less frequent themes of myrrh and vineyards, respectively, with those more prominent ones of wine and ships.

I Wine and Myrrh

Many of Alcaeus's poems are exhortations to drinking—which in the Greek world meant the drinking of wine. These references to drinking may be conveniently analyzed in terms of the functions Alcaeus assigns wine in his poems and of the vocabulary and moods with which drinking is associated.[1] Alcaeus's world is the world of the symposium and partisan camaraderie,[2] and we may take as our point of departure the fact that he treats drinking as the first and most natural expression of joy. This is implied in the meager remains of Z 78 with its boisterous imperatives "be happy and drink" and is even more emphatically expressed in the gleeful announcement of the death of a tyrant who was also a hated political opponent ("Myrsilus Is Dead!" = Z 8): "Now's the time to get drunk and with some vigor/ to drink, for Myrsilus has died, indeed he has ..." Too, the joyful announcement that spring is in bloom is followed directly by the

50

order to "mix as quickly as you can a bowl of the honey-sweet" ("Spring" = Z 44; "the honey-sweet" is an epithet for wine). It is, however, not clear from the one surviving line of "Dinnomenes" (Z 53) whether drinking is the expression of joy or only associated with a pleasant situation: "You empty a cup, sitting beside Dinnomenes." Still, it is clear that in "Dinnomenes" wine drinking is at least a means of enjoyment, if not the expression of joy. It is surely the means rather than the expression in "Sisyphus" (B 6 A). This poem begins with the injunction "Drink with me, Melanippus" and then turns to morbid speculation about the inevitability of death (lines 2-10). We may summarize the mood of the poem as follows. Death is certain. Let us enjoy life while we can. We may do so, Melanippus, by drinking.

It is as a means of enjoyment that wine functions as a panacea for the anxieties, misfortunes, and discomforts of human existence. Indeed, the drinking enjoined in "Sisyphus" nebulously assumes the function of an antidote to anxiety, for hovering behind the actual words of the poem is the subtle implication that a man can drink away the fear of death. The matter is more bluntly stated in "Wine" (Z 11): in the midst of calamity and grief, Alcaeus advises Bycchis, "the best of medicines/ is to bring in the wine and get drunk." Equally blunt is "Let Us Drink" (Z 22), which begins with the exhortation "Let us drink! Why wait for the lamps?" and includes orders for an inordinately strong mixture.[3] It also gives a reason for heavy drinking (lines 3-4): "Wine's the duller-of-grief the son of Zeus and Semele/ gave to men."

In addition, Alcaeus extends the curative powers of wine to even the ordinary discomforts of life. The description of a hot and enervating summer begins "Soak your lungs with wine, for the dog-star's in the sky" ("Summer" = Z 23, line 1); and the relation of drinking to physical discomfort was probably similar in Z 29, whose only preserved words are "Let's drink, for the dog-star's in the sky." Winter too is to be dealt with by heavy drinking. A description of stormy, freezing weather ("Winter" = Z 14, lines 1-4) is followed by a prescription for conquering the winter storm: build up the fire, mix great quantities of honey-sweet wine (lines 5-7).

Several other references to wine invite speculation or examination, though absolute conclusions are ruled out, since in each instance the surrounding context is either not preserved or in a highly mutilated condition. It may be that the "honey-sweet wine" and "wine sharper than thistles" of Z 46 represent respectively good times and bad times, the latter referring to the vinegar at the bottom of the storage jar.[4] It may be instead, however, that Alcaeus is merely extolling the benefits of wine, saying that bad wine is better than no wine at all. Or it may be, we must admit, that both explanations are wrong and that the absence of context puts even probable explanation completely beyond our grasp. This is likely to be the situation with Z 35, where there *seems* to be a reference to wine's shackling someone's mind (line 1). If this is an accurate interpretation of the reference—and I stress that the line in which it occurs is very mutilated—then it is the only circumstance among all the fragments when wine is depicted as a bad thing.

We may conclude this examination of Alcaeus's references to wine and drinking by speculating about the relation between a pair of one line fragments that are widely separated in source. What sort of truth did Alcaeus have in mind when he wrote "wine, dear boy, and truth" (Z 43)? The answer is perhaps provided by Z 9: "wine's a window opening into a man." It is through drinking with a man that you learn what he is really like, that you learn the truth about his character.[5]

The extant fragments lead us to conclude that Alcaeus never extended his moral vision beyond a world of masculine camaraderie and partisan politics, a world of loyalty to faction and sympotic fellowship. Yet within the narrow confines of Alcaeus's poetic *cosmos,* wine is a lofty and beneficent sign, conferring whatever of joy and comfort this world has to offer. Alcaeus perhaps sums up his attitude toward wine when he urges (Z 18) "And don't raise any other plant before the vine."

The poetic function of myrrh is similar, though the references to it are far fewer and, of course, equally fragmentary. Joy seems to be the keynote of "Dill and Myrrh" (Z 39), where, after ordering plaited necklaces of dill, Alcaeus adds "and let him pour sweet myrrh over our chests." It is, however, comfort that is requested in "The Plea" (B 18, lines 1-2): "Over my head (for I have suffered much) pour myrrh/ and over my hoary chest. . . . " And the similarity between wine and myrrh is not limited to poetic function, for they share epithets indicating sweetness: in "Dill and Myrrh" (Z 39) myrrh is "sweet," and wine is twice called the "honey-sweet" ("Spring" = Z 44, line 2; Z 46).

II *Ships and Vineyards*

One of Alcaeus's favorite images is the storm-racked ship. There is, moreover, substantial evidence that Alcaeus's ship images, or a least some of them, are more than simple images, that they have an allegorical function and are to be related to Alcaeus's partisan involvement in the political turmoil of his city-state Mytilene. It is my purpose in this section to analyze these ship-in-storm images in terms of their possible allegorical meaning. The fragmentary state of Alcaeus's poetry accounts for the word "possible" in the previous sentence and precludes the assumption that any of these ship images *must* be taken a priori as allegorical.[6] My methodology will be, first, to establish categories of evidence, and then to examine each category. This should give my readers an objective criterion—and one that is quite apart from my own conclusions and assessment of the evidence—for determining the allegorical element, or lack of it, in a given image. Before setting up these categories, however, it seems critically appropriate to make some introductory observations about nautical imagery in Greek poetry prior to Alcaeus.

Nautical imagery was well established in this earlier poetry.[7] One may cite, for example, the elaborate description in book five of the *Odyssey* of the storm which tossed Odysseus ashore in the land of the Phaeacians. Or a simile such as that in book fifteen of the *Iliad* (lines 379-85):[8]

> But the Trojans, hearing the thunderstroke of Zeus
> of the aegis,
> remembered even more their warcraft, and sprang
> on the Argives.
> They, as when the big waves on the sea wide-
> wandering
> wash across the walls of a ship underneath
> the leaning
> force of the wind, which particularly piles
> up the big waves,
> so the Trojans with huge clamor went over the
> rampart
> and drove their horses to fight alongside the
> grounded vessels.

There is, furthermore, in this pre-Alcaean period one example of a marine allegory, though it does *not* involve a ship. For we are informed by an ancient critic that the following verses by Archilochus, whose date is uncertain but who certainly died no later than 640 B.C., constitute an allegory:[9] "Glaukos, look! The open sea is churning to a wash of waves/ deep within. A cloud stands upright over the Gyrean cape,/ signal of a storm, and terror rises from the unforeseen." The ancient critic observes that in this allegory the heavy seas represent war.

There is not, however, in this prior literature an instance of an image in which a ship symbolizes the state or a political coterie within the state.[10] On the other hand, such an allegorical image is extremely common in Greek literature after Alcaeus[11] and is employed by Alcaeus's literary heir Horace in Book I, 14 of his *Odes*. (And it might be added that the allegory in question has become a commonplace of Western literature.) In asking ourselves whether or not and, if so, to what extent Alcaeus employed an allegory of the storm-racked ship, we are, therefore, dealing with a question fundamental to his poetic originality. For if Alcaeus employed this allegory, his is the first extant example of it in Greco-Roman literature; and he is primarily and directly responsible for its occurrence in Horace's highly influential *Odes* I, 14. [12]

As for the categories mentioned above, the pertinent evidence may be classified as either external or internal. The external evidence is in the form of explanatory statements about Alcaeus's poetry made by unknown Greek commentators and by an obscure Heraclitus, who wrote, perhaps in the first century A.D., a work cited as either *Allegories* or *Homeric Questions*. The remarks of the commentators are badly preserved and are designated as V 1 (column ii), X (14), and X (16) in Lobel and Page's edition of the fragments of Sappho and Alcaeus. The other category of evidence, the internal evidence, is subjective and is based on an analysis of the poems in which Alcaeus uses ship imagery. It should be stressed that the external evidence was itself originally subjective and analytical, for neither a commentator nor Heraclitus had before him an explanation by Alcaeus that a ship was being used as an allegorical image. The ancient interpreter of Alcaeus, however, was working with whole poems, while his modern counterpart has at his disposal only enigmatic pieces of poems. And therein is the reason that we must not ignore the remarks of Heraclitus and the commentators.

Let us now test each of Alcaeus's ship images that can be viewed as possibly allegorical against the categorical touchstones just set up and see what the results are. We may begin with "The Ship: II" (Z 2 + V 1.ii + K 5 [a] ii), whose extant remains depict a ship caught in a storm and being torn apart by wind and wave.[13] Heraclitus quotes the first nine lines of this poem—that is, its entire Z 2 portion—to illustrate his statement that Alcaeus often uses allegories in which the turmoil occasioned by political tyranny corresponds to a stormy condition at sea.[14] Heraclitus adds immediately that a hasty reader might miss the allegory in the vivid storm image but that it is there, since Alcaeus is alluding to the tyrannical conspiracy of Myrsilus against the Mytileneans. Also, it is likely but not certain both that V 1, column ii is a commentary on "The Ship: II" and that one of the comments refers to Myrsilus (line 8).

The external evidence. therefore, is emphatically in favor of allegory. Yet, Heraclitus's remark that the hasty reader might miss the allegory gives one pause and recommends an examination of the poem itself. (I will leave out of consideration its K 5 portion as being too fragmentary to offer anything more than obfuscation to the present inquiry.) The surviving verses of "The Ship: II" contain no explicit indication of allegory, only a description of a ship which is about to be swamped by waves and whose sail is in tatters. There is, however, a striking piece of internal evidence that must be taken into consideration. Alcaeus describes the storm in the first person and present tense as though it were actually taking place and he were actually on the foundering vessel: "I am confused by the clash of winds" (line 1), the waves are surging on both sides and we in their midst are being carried along on our dark ship (lines 2-4), and the bilge is above the masthold (line 6). What is being depicted is either a past event, a creation of Alcaeus's poetic imagination, or a combination of both; and the use of the vivid present in such circumstances lends credibility to Heraclitus's allegorical exegesis. Still the internal evidence for allegory that is available to us—and we must not forget that Heraclitus had before him a whole poem—is scarcely sufficient to *demand* the presence of allegory. Indeed, in her famous Fragment 31 ("Fortunate as the gods he seems to me, that man who sits opposite you, and listens nearby to your sweet voice"),[15] Sappho employs the vivid present to describe an event that is either past, or the creation of her poetic imagination, or a combination of both; and yet there is no reason to treat this vivid present as a sign of allegory. Also, in the obviously nonallegorical "The Prayer" (G 1) Alcaeus vividly and dramatically portrays himself as actually praying to specific deities. The internal evidence for allegory in "The Ship: II" (Z 2) must, therefore, be classified as neutral.

In the case of "The Ship: I" (A 6) the internal evidence is more cogent, while the external evidence remains equally as compelling. Heraclitus quotes the first three lines of this poem (they reveal that Alcaeus's ship is about to be struck by a huge wave) with the explanation that in them Alcaeus is enigmatically referring to the times of Myrsilus.[16] He then comments that Alcaeus uses sea imagery to excess in his allegories and symbolizes as storms at sea the majority of the evils due to tyrants.

"The Ship: I" is also composed in the vivid present: another wave is about to strike our ship (lines 1-2); it will require great labor for us to bail out the water (lines 2-3); let us run for a secure harbor (line 8). In addition, there is substantial internal evidence for allegory in the third and fourth stanzas, which, though mutilated, are complete enough to permit analysis. From these stanzas (lines 9-16) we can extract, either explicitly or implicitly, the following exhortations: let no man play the coward (lines 9-10); remember your former prowess (line 11); let every man win the approval of his comrades (line 12); let us not disgrace our noble ancestors lying under the earth (lines 13-14). Though some guesswork is involved in lines 11 and 12, it is still obvious that these exhortations are more appropriate to preparation for battle—whether against a foreign enemy or in civil war—than to behavior on board a ship caught in a storm.[17]

These exhortations impress me as a transition from allegory to a passage in which the allegory is somehow explained, and the appearance of the words "ancestors" (line 17) and "monarchy" (line 27) in the later and more fragmented verses of the poem tends to corroborate this impression. In view of this general thematic development after verse 8, verse 8 itself ("and to a secure harbor let us run") deserves further consideration. The adjective "secure" is equally appropriate to a harbor and to a military position on land. "Let us run," however, which directly precedes the two transitional stanzas (lines 9-16), is literally appropriate to a movement by soldiers on land and only metaphorically suitable to a maneuver by a ship. Having classified verses 9-16 as a passage providing a transition from allegory, I would regard verse 8 as a subtle hint that the transition is to begin—or, if you will, as a transition to the transition. There is not enough Greek preserved to permit us to understand how Alcaeus extricated himself from the transition proper, but we can trace his gradual movement into it: from "secure" to "let us run" to exhortations which no longer fit the allegory in any way. By the end of verse nine the careful reader realizes that the storm-racked ship is not to be taken literally and that the poem has departed from its opening image.

Both the external and the internal evidence become more tenuous and more difficult to assess when we move on to the other poems containing nautical imagery. In the case of "The Ship: II" (Z 2) and "The Ship: I" (A 6), although the poems were fragmentary and incomplete, Heraclitus's comments—that is, the external evidence—were clear and well preserved. The other ship imagery that we must examine for evidence of allegory is in poems equally or even more fragmentary; but now the external evidence is either nonexistent or else in the form of explanations by unknown commentators, whose observations are themselves so ill preserved as to permit only the broadest and most elementary conclusions.

"The Reef" (D 15) opens with a description of a storm-battered ship (lines 1-6). The external evidence for allegory is furnished by an ancient commentator, who is explaining Alcaeus's reference to an unmarked reef in lines 5-6 of the poem.[18] The full substance of this explanation is mutilated beyond even speculation, but it does afford in lines 11-13 a reference to an author "who likes to use allegory." From what is preserved of this commentary on "The Reef" (D 15), we may conclude that this allegorizing author is either Anacreon or Alcaeus and that the commentator believed that Alcaeus's unmarked reef had allegorical significance. It is, furthermore, likely that the commentator ranged more widely in his exegesis of the poem and assigned allegorical functions also to the ship and the stormy sea. The external evidence, therefore, despite its fragmentary state, should be classified as supportive of allegory. *Mutatis mutandis* the same may be said of the internal evidence.

The description of the storm-racked ship is in the present tense (lines 1-7) and is followed by what seems to be an exhortation to merrymaking and to forgetting about the difficulties the ship is in (lines 8-10). Such an exhortation is appropriate only to an allegorical ship and is reminiscent of the exhortations of "The Ship: I" (A 6), which have already been explained as indicative not of a real ship in a real storm but of their allegorical counterparts.

I have concluded that both external and internal evidence are in favor of an allegorical interpretation of "The Reef" (D 15), and I have stated this conclusion with some certainty. At the same time, I would be less than honest with my reader if I did not grant that the restoration of the full poem and all the commentary might well disrupt this certainty.[19]

At this point in our discussion external and internal evidence cease to overlap. The commentator of X (14), column ii, is clearly analyzing an Alcaean ship as an allegorical image (see especially lines 17-21), but not enough of the commentary is preserved to reveal either what the ship symbolizes or in what poem it appears.[20] And there is no external evidence whatsoever for the allegorical possibilities of "Foresight" (L 1) and "Castor and Polydeuces" (B 2 [a]). Nevertheless, the nautical imagery of these two poems shares certain common features with that previously examined for indications of allegory, and it is only logical to classify both poems as allegorical candidates and to analyze them for internal evidence of allegory.

The mutilated portions (lines 1-5 and 10-13) of "Foresight" (L 1) contain references to a ship and to wind, while sandwiched between this mutilated material is a statement to the effect that one should make adequate preparations for a voyage before setting sail but that after he is at sea he must adjust to whatever circumstances arise (lines 6-9). In the light of the nautical imagery previously discussed, I would conclude that "Foresight" (L 1) contained a description, in the present tense, of a ship caught in rough seas, together with some general advice about how to deal with the situation. The general advice about preparations before a voyage and behavior at sea impresses me as somewhat less than poetically credible in a description of a real nautical situation and as more appropriate to an allegorical than to a real voyage.[21] I am, therefore, inclined to put this advice in the same category as the exhortations of "The Ship:

I" (A 6) and "The Reef" (D 15) and to view the internal evidence of "Foresight" (L 1) as indicative of allegory.

The last poem under scrutiny for evidence of allegory is "Castor and Polydeuces" (B 2 [a]). As already pointed out, there is no external evidence that this poem should be interpreted allegorically. Furthermore, were it not for the mass of external and internal evidence for nautical allegory that has been presented and analyzed in connection with other poems, there would be no justification for examining "Castor and Polydeuces" (B 2 [a]) for internal indications of allegory. In my opinion, however, the amassed evidence is sufficient for the conclusion that Alcaeus is prone to employ nautical imagery in an allegorical sense and that any description of a ship caught in a storm must be approached as at least a possible candidate for allegory.

From the extant remains of "Castor and Polydeuces" (B 2 [a]) we can determine with assurance that the poem is cast in the form of a hymn to this beneficent pair, sons of Zeus and Leda, who are often designated by the patronymic Dioscuri ("sons of Zeus") and who rescue mariners from death at sea. The Dioscuri were the subject of a Homeric Hymn (number 33), which is roughly contemporary with Alcaeus's poem, and of a hymn by Theocritus (Idyll 22), a Greek poet of the early Hellenistic period; and Alcaeus's poem shares with these two hymns certain features crucial for determining its literary form.[22] All three poems open with invocations of the Dioscuri, in which they are addressed as Castor and Polydeuces, designated as sons of Zeus and Leda, and assigned the Peloponnesus as their homeland. Also, all three poems indicate that the Dioscuri traverse land and sea on horseback, calming stormy seas and rescuing sailors from death. And despite the fact that Alcaeus's hymn is composed in the vivid present (as is revealed by the urgent imperative "appear" in verse three), it may be that it is no more than a purely literary endeavor employing a popular poetic form.

Much uncertainty, however, remains. After the invocation of the Dioscuri (lines 1-4) and a description of their customary, beneficent activities (lines 5-12)—namely, that they ride over land and sea bearing succor to mariners in distress and manifesting themselves as Saint Elmo's fire[23]—the poem breaks off, and there is not the slightest textual hint as to what succeeded. At the same time, the hymn opened with an urgent appeal for the

Dioscuri to appear (lines 1-3); and in view of this appeal, we must assume that Alcaeus went on to describe in the vivid present a storm in which his ship is foundering.[24] It may further be that, even within the hymnal framework of the poem, the ship and the storm had allegorical significance. This last point, however, is scarcely subject to proof, since only the first stanzas of Alcaeus's hymn are extant. It seems reasonable to conclude, therefore, that the internal evidence for allegory in "Castor and Polydeuces" (B 2 [a]) is confined to the fact that this poem depicted in the vivid present a ship in distress. Such nautical imagery in other poems, where there is evidence adequate for a decision as to its symbolic function, consistently requires an allegorical explanation.

By now it has become apparent that I am sympathetic with the allegorical interpretation of Alcaeus's nautical imagery, but before turning to the question of what the allegorical images symbolize, I would like to summarize my critical reaction to the evidence for allegory that has been presented and analyzed. As for the external evidence, especially the comments of Heraclitus, *no* internal evidence has been found to refute it, and much has come to light to support it, primarily the exhortations of "The Ship: I" (A 6) and "The Reef" (D 15) and the general advice of "Foresight" (L 1). In view of this situation and because Heraclitus and the unknown commentators were basing their allegorical interpretations on complete rather than fragmentary poems, the modern critic can do no better than to accept the fact of allegory in Alcaeus's nautical imagery. This does not mean, however, that every nautical image introduced by Alcaeus is to be allegorically explained, for a priori the only allegorical possibilities involved a storm-racked ship. Nor does it mean that every ship-in-storm image *must* be regarded as an allegory. It is, however, my personal belief that all nautical imagery considered in this section should be classified as allegorical, with the possible exception of that in "Castor and Poly-deuces" (B 2 [a]). The hesitation and subjectivism in which this conclusion is couched and which has run throughout the previous analysis of the evidence for allegory is an unavoidable by-product of interpreting a poet as fragmentary as Alcaeus.

Having concluded that the allegorical exegesis of Alcaeus's ship-in-storm images is a legitimate critical endeavor, it remains for me to analyze the symbolism of the allegories—that is, to explain what real things the various elements in the allegories stand for. As always, the fragmentary state of Alcaeus's poetry causes difficulties. With Heraclitus's help, however, it is possible to establish certain basic premises on which to build an analysis of Alcaeus's nautical symbolism.

The first such premise is that there is a substantial amount of nonallegorical detail within the allegories and that allegorical symbolism must not be demanded of every element within the description of a storm-racked ship. Heraclitus implies as much, when, after quoting the first nine verses of "The Ship: II" (Z 2), he adds: "Who at first glance would not think, because of the extensive sea imagery, that Alcaeus is describing fear at sea on the part of real mariners? This, however, is not the case; for Myrsilus is meant, and a tyrannical conspiracy that is being formed against the Mytileneans."[25] Alcaeus, therefore, is always the poet; and, even when allegorizing, he strives for vivid and striking imagery, even to the extent of—or perhaps even for the purpose of—disguising the presence of allegory. Exclusive of this nonallegorical detail, we must reckon with three allegorical elements whose symbolism requires explanation: the storm, the ship (together with those on board), and the voyage.

The second premise is likewise derived from Heraclitus. It is that the three symbols in each nautical allegory represent fundamentally the same thing. Heraclitus quotes the first nine verses of "The Ship: II" (Z 2) to illustrate his twofold point that Alcaeus frequently employs allegory and that in his allegories he equates the political turmoil caused by tyrants with a stormy condition at sea. He then identifies the imminent tyranny of Myrsilus as that symbolized by the storm of "The Ship: II" (Z 2) and cites "The Ship: I" (A 6) as another poem in which Myrsilus's tyranny is allegorized as a storm at sea. Finally, Heraclitus offers the summarizing remark that Alcaeus "represents the majority of the evils occasioned by tyrants as storms at sea." The storm in Alcaeus's nautical allegories, therefore, symbolizes the political evils of a tyranny. In "The Ship: II" (Z 2) and "The Ship: I" (A 6) the tyrant in question is Myrsilus. Heraclitus's reference to "the evils occasioned by tyrants," however, indicates that other tyrannies may be involved in other poems. For practical purposes this means that we cannot be sure whose tyranny is symbolized by the storms of "The Reef" (D 15), "Foresight" (L 1), and "Castor and

Polydeuces" (B 2 [a]), if indeed this last poem is allegorical.
Nevertheless, we can do no better than follow Heraclitus and
conclude that in Alcaeus's nautical allegories the storm at sea
always symbolizes the political evils of a tyranny, even if the
tyrant in question is not always identifiable.

Having established that the storm has only one fundamental
symbolism throughout all the nautical allegories, it is both reasonable and consistent to apply the same principle to the other
two elements, the ship (together with those on board) and the
voyage, and to set up as a basic premise that the identification of
the symbolism of an element in one allegory necessarily implies
its identification in all the allegories. Still, we must not be too
precise in our fundamental identifications, for in demonstrating
that storms at sea represent the political evils of a tyranny we
discovered that the tyrant may vary from poem to poem.

In the process of justifying the second of the basic premises,
the fundamental signification of the storm was established. Let
us next turn to the ship and its crew. That Alcaeus and his
comrades are conceived of as the crew and not merely passengers
is indicated by the fact that in "The Ship: I" (A 6) they will bail
out the vessel after the next wave strikes (lines 1-3)—that is,
they will behave and function as its crew. Also, that they are
conceived of as Mytilenean sailors is indicated in the same poem
by the exhortation of verses 13-14: "Let us not disgrace our
noble forefathers lying under the earth." Since Alcaeus is himself a Mytilenean, it could only be fellow Mytileneans that he
is addressing in such words. The allegorical image, therefore,
is of a ship manned by Mytilenean sailors and struggling against
a storm. Since the storm always symbolizes the political evils
of a tyranny, we cannot but conclude that the ship with its
crew represents a political party struggling against this tyranny,
whether it be that of Myrsilus or of some other tyrant. Since
Myrsilus (or whatever tyrant is intended in a given poem)
and his followers are Mytileneans too, the ship and crew cannot symbolize the state as a whole with all its citizenry—
except in the sense that, say, de Gaulle and the "Free French"
regarded themselves as the true France during World War II.
Though Alcaeus may well regard his party as the true polis of
Mytilene, in fact the ship and crew of the allegory must represent only that part of the state sharing Alcaeus's political
persuasion. It is a ship of party rather than a ship of state.

That the ship as we have it lacks a captain may or may not be due to the accidents of fragmentary preservation. It is, however, idle to speculate in what poems or under what circumstances such a captain may have been mentioned or designated by name, for there is at present neither external nor internal evidence to guide us.

By now it is becoming obvious that the voyage, the last of the three allegorical elements, in some way represents the political course taken by Alcaeus's party. Whether a particular course of action or merely the general activity of this party is symbolized by the voyage is uncertain in "The Ship: II" (Z 2), "The Reef" (D 15), and, if it is to be classified as allegorical, "Castor and Polydeuces" (B 2 [a]). The extant portions of these poems give no indication that Alcaeus has in mind a specific military or political enterprise; yet there is always the frustrating possibility that such a specific enterprise was alluded to in the lost verses of all or any of these poems. (And we must not overlook the possibility that Alcaeus's practice in this regard varied from poem to poem.) Moreover, the reference in "Foresight" (L 1) to making adequate preparations for a voyage while on land but adjusting to circumstance after setting sail (lines 6-9) indicates that at least in this poem Alcaeus was allegorizing a rather specific course of action. In addition, in "The Ship: I" (A 6) the exhortations to bravery and to not disgracing one's ancestors (lines 9-14)—exhortations strikingly appropriate to preparations for battle—reveal that the voyage of this poem is a particular military enterprise, conceivably even that mentioned as "this task" in the last line of "The Armory" (Z 34).

In summary, in Alcaeus's nautical allegories the storm symbolizes the political evils of a tyranny; the ship with its crew Alcaeus's party, which is struggling against the tyrant; and the voyage the course of action, whether specific or general, taken by this party. Such allegories are exclusively political, and their symbolism is entirely consistent with what we know of Alcaeus's partisan involvement in the political affairs of Mytilene.

There remains for analysis the single nonnautical allegory, whose fragments constitute the best preserved verses of "The Vineyard" (F 5).[26] Although there is no external evidence for allegory in this poem, it is my conviction that the tone of its last three stanzas (lines 9-20) demands for them an allegorical explanation and that a description of what remains of this poem will be sufficient demonstration of that fact. The first two stanzas are too fragmentary to permit the decipherment of even their general content, but it is noteworthy for present interests that there is in them no indication of allegory. The first two verses of the next stanza are complete (lines 9-10): "For already is your time past/ and all the fruit has been gathered." There follow successively references to a fair shoot that hopefully will bear "not a few clusters of grapes" (lines 11-12) and to something (apparently the harvest of grapes) that will come "from such a vine as this" (lines 13-14). Next, two complete verses in which Alcaeus states his fear that "they will pluck" the grapes before they ripen (lines 15-16; it is impossible to identify the "they" who will do the plucking); and finally, after an obscure reference to "those who previously labored" (line 17), only incomprehensible groups of letters.

The nautical allegories were presented in the first person and the present tense; and viticulture, discussed in these tones, and incorporated into a poem written in the first person and present tense (reference to "me," line 6; "I fear," line 15), cannot but have allegorical signification. At the same time, the symbolism of the elements of this allegory is beyond our grasp, for we have absolutely no means for determining precisely what is represented by the vine with its clusters of grapes and fair shoot or by the two groups that are mentioned, those who may pluck the grapes and those who have previously labored. Nevertheless, the tone of this allegory and the symbolism of the nautical allegories combine to assure us that the viticultural allegory of "The Vineyard" (F 5) is political in reference and connotation, even if we cannot define what is specifically represented by each element of the allegory.

It is also possible to learn something about Alcaeus's poetic techniques by examining the manner in which he has incorporated the viticultural allegory into the framework of the poem. As I have already argued, the first two stanzas of "The Vineyard" (F 5) are nonallegorical; and the allegory begins with the third stanza. As I see the poem, the first two verses of this stanza provide the transition from the real to the allegorical situation ("For already is your time past/ and all the fruit has been gathered," lines 9-10). The signification of "your time" in verse 9 and of "all the fruit" in the next verse is similar, if not identical. The unidentifiable *you* of line 9 (it is singular) is, therefore, the key transitional word, for it belongs both to the preceding reality and to the following allegory. The reader begins verse 9 in the midst of a real situation, and by the end of verse 9 he is fully involved in an allegorical one.

We have thus been able to trace the transition from the non-allegorical to the allegorical portion of "The Vineyard" (F 5). The poem, however, is too fragmentary after its fourth stanza to allow us to determine how, or even if, Alcaeus extricated himself from the allegory. This situation is somewhat analogous to that in which we found ourselves when analyzing "The Ship: I" (A 6). In that poem we were able to trace the beginning and some of the body of Alcaeus's carefully plotted transition from the nautical allegory into a nonallegorical portion of the poem, but readable text failed us in the midst of the transition and we could not see how it was completed.

Despite such uncertainties, what we have been able to discern about the structure of "The Ship: I" (A 6) and "The Vineyard" (F 5) is, from a broad perspective, critically instructive. It teaches us that Alcaeus did not feel compelled to write allegorical poems that were allegorical in their entirety. And this lesson in turn raises the question whether Alcaeus ever wrote poems that were truly and fully allegorical or whether he only inserted allegories into poems that were politically motivated. The apparent exhortation to merrymaking in the third stanza of "The Reef" (D 15) puts this poem in the latter category. Of the six allegorical candidates, therefore, half demonstrably use an allegory only as an imaginal unit within a longer poem. And in each case there are indications that the nonallegorical portion of the poem went far toward explaining the allegory. All this creates the general impression that Alcaeus's allegories would not be difficult to decipher, if only the poems in which they occur were not so fragmentary.

CHAPTER 5

Similes and Metaphors

IN addition to the elaborate and extended metaphors which constitute the allegories just discussed, Alcaeus employs a number of similes and metaphors that comment on his literary techniques and help define his poetic vision. The scant remains of "The Smoldering Log" (D 16) would permit no judgment as to its content, were it not for a marginal comment on "the log," which are the only surviving words of verse 6, and "sends forth only," which is all that remains of verse 7. (The fragments of the poem taken by themselves are not sufficient to reveal whether "the log" is the subject of "sends forth," its object or, indeed, whether there is no syntactical connection between the two phrases.) The scholiast offers a figurative interpretation of Alcaeus's reference to "the log" together with some summary of its surrounding context:[1] "But, oh men of Mytilene, while the log still sends off only smoke—that is, while he is not yet a tyrant—put it out and put a stop to it quickly, that its fire may not become brighter."

It is clear from this comment that in Alcaeus's figure the log is the subject of "sends forth" and that it represents a prospective tyrant on the verge of seizing power. What is not clear, however, is whether the figure is a simile, a metaphor, or an allegory of the type examined in the previous chapter. Some support for the last mentioned classification is afforded by the scholiast's insertion of "oh men of Mytilene" in his comment, for the manner of its insertion indicates that Alcaeus employed a similar vocative in his poem and that the Mytileneans so addressed played a role both in Alcaeus's figure and in the surrounding, nonfigurative context. In fact, the poem as a whole may well be an admonition addressed to these "men of Mytilene," since the legible portion of a scholion to verse 4 reads, "But you are silent . . . completely unable to resist the tyrant." Alcaeus, therefore, employed, in the midst of an admonition directed to his fellow countrymen, a figure in which these same countrymen represented themselves. This technique of locking the figurative to the real situation by means of an element shared in common has already been remarked in the case of the allegories. In "The Vineyard" (F 5) we observed that the unidentifiable *you* of line 9 belongs to the real as well as to the figurative situation, and in "The Ship: I" (A 6) the Mytileneans who are exhorted in the transition from the figurative to the real situation (lines 9-16) are also the allegorical crew of the allegorical ship whose difficulties have just been depicted (lines 1-8). Since the figure used in "The Smoldering Log" (D 16) is linked to the real circumstances of the poem by means of a technique used to link these two allegorical figures to the real circumstances they symbolize, it is possible that the log of "The Smoldering Log" was actually only one element in an allegory which Alcaeus developed at some length.

The succinctness of the scholiast's explanation, however, militates against this classification, just as the very nature of his summary makes that of simile somewhat less than likely. My inclination is to classify Alcaeus's figure as a brief, implied metaphor, in which the smoldering log that the Mytileneans are urged to extinguish represents a tyrant ready to seize power. In a figure of this sort, the inclusion of the Mytileneans in both the real and the metaphorical situation would be quite natural—indeed, it seems almost unavoidable. When Alcaeus uses a shared element to link an allegory with its complex of metaphors to the real circumstances it symbolizes, he is doing no more than applying a literary technique native to the brief and simple metaphor.

The metaphor of the smoldering log has to it a ring of the popular and proverbial, and it belongs to a large group of similar metaphors and similes. Such is the figurative allusion to the stone of Tantalus in the single verse that constitutes "The Stone of Tantalus" (Z 42): "There lies above your head, O son of Aesimus, a great stone." The stone must here represent some chronic and terrible danger, as it did when previously used by Archilochus (Fragment 55): "Let not the stone of Tantalus hang over this island."[2]

Several of these popular and proverbial figures employ a bestial motif. Our sources inform us that the sow of Z 70 ("again the sow provokes"; this statement is the sum total of the frag-

ment) represents a troublemaker;[3] and in "The Fox" (D 11) a
man attempting a shrewd diplomatic or political maneuver is
likened to a "fox of crafty mind" (lines 6-8). Though it is uncertain whom or what sort of person the she-goat of Scyros represents (Z 112), there is no doubt that the reference occurred
in a simile or metaphor of proverbial tone.[4] Similar in tone is the
metaphorical equation of a man with his money, which Alcaeus
acknowledges he borrowed from Aristodemus ("A Saying of
Aristodemus" = Z 37): "money's the man, and no poor man is
any good or held in honor."

Equally proverbial but far more complex in thought are three
other figures. The first (Z 20) and second (Z 28) are implied
metaphors, but the prose context in which the third (Z 115) is
preserved makes it impossible to determine whether it is a
metaphor or a simile. The scholiast who has recorded the proverbial metaphor of "The Headache" (Z 20), which is all that
remains of this poem, has offered no explanation as to what
real circumstances Alcaeus has in mind when he refers to getting a headache by moving a certain kind of stone. We, however,
will not go far astray if we accept C. M. Bowra's decipherment
that Alcaeus is referring "to some ill-chosen task which will bring
trouble to him who undertakes it."[5] The commentator who
quotes the verse and a half that make up Z 28 indicates that
Alcaeus was borrowing a metaphor from the game of draughts
when he referred to a man who prevailed by moving the stone
from the sacred line. In draughts this particular move is chosen
only as a last resort by a player in desperate circumstances.[6]
Again, the source of Z 115, a reference by Alcaeus to drawing the
lion from his claw, reveals that this is a figure that alludes to
pursuing great things with small but adequate resources.[7]

The use of bestial motifs in popular and sometimes earthy
metaphors of the type we have just been examining was well
established in Greek nonepic poetry prior to Alcaeus, for they
are employed in abundance by Archilochus and Semonides,
both of whom wrote early enough to have influenced Alcaeus.
Indeed, Alcaeus's "fox of crafty mind" ("The Fox" = D 11, lines
6-8) is reminiscent of and may well have been inspired by the
"clever fox with shrewd mind" who appears along with a monkey
in one of Archilochus's allegorical fables (81). Archilochus elsewhere introduces a fox and an eagle (89) and a fox and a
hedgehog (103), and in the simile of 18 an island is compared

to a donkey ("Here the island stands/ stiff with wild timber like a donkey's bristling back").[8] It should be noted that in each but the last of these Archilochean figures there is the same proverbial ring that we have already detected in many of Alcaeus's figures. It is an earthy tone, however, that prevails in Semonides's long poem designating and describing all the types of women.[9] The types are variously represented by a sow, a vixen, a bitch, the earth, the sea, a donkey, a weasel, a mare, a monkey, and the one good type by a bee.

So much for the popular and proverbial aspect of Alcaeus's bestiary. Several of the beast figures have a distinctively epic tone. Though the epithet Alcaeus applies to himself in line 25 of "Exile" (G 2) is fraught with etymological uncertainties, it is clear that the general import of the word is that Alcaeus is forced to live like a wolf;[10] and the linguistic composition of Alcaeus's epithet is similar to that of the Homeric "wolf-born," which is twice applied to Apollo in the *Iliad* (Book IV, lines 101 and 119). The very fact that no particular beast is designated in two implied metaphors adds to the figure a dimension of horror and monstrosity. In "Pittacus" (D 12) Alcaeus says sardonically of the subject of the poem, "Let him devour the city even as he did with Myrsilus" (line 7); and in "The Prayer" (G 1) he writes of this same Pittacus: "indifferently with his paws/ he trampled on his oaths and now devours/ the city ..." (lines 22-24).[11] Homer uses the verb *devour* in its literal sense only of animals devouring their prey: of a lion or ravening jackals devouring a stag (*Iliad*, Book XI, lines 474-81); of ravening wolves, their mouths dripping with blood, devouring a stag (Book XVI, lines 156-63); of dogs devouring a dead man (Book XXIII, lines 182-83). The Alcaean image is of a wild animal glutting itself on a whole city. It is also reminiscent of Homer's "people-devouring king" (*dēmoboros basileus*, a title contemptuously flung at Agamemnon by Achilles at *Iliad*, Book VII, line 231), just as Alcaeus's "spirit-devouring sedition" (*thymoboros lya*) at line 10 of "Pittacus" (D 12) calls to mind Homer's recurrent "spirit-devouring strife" (*thymoboros eris*).

The deer frequently appears in Homeric similes, and there is in Alcaeus's "Lady of Misery" (A 10) an enigmatically fragmentary figure (lines 5-7) which contains a reference to a deer. In the first stanza of the poem a woman is lamenting her misery and misfortune, though there is no preserved indication as to the nature of her misfortune or to whether she is a historical person, a fictional creation by Alcaeus, or a character of either folk-lore or legend. The figure in question, which opens the second stanza of the poem, is obviously a simile or a metaphor involving the phrase "in the fearful heart" as well as references to a deer (it is uncertain whether it is male or female) and to the roar or cry of an animal. The enigma posed by the ill-preserved state of the figure has aroused considerable critical speculation.

To my knowledge, the roar or cry (Greek *bromos*) has always been attributed to the deer, so that the figure would begin "and the belling of a deer" (line 5; the translation is of *elaphō de bromos*). It is uncertain whether "the fearful heart" (line 5) belongs to a hind or to the woman uttering the complaint. If the deer is a stag, the "fearful heart" would belong to a hind and the verse would then be translated either as "and the belling of a stag causes to grow in her fearful heart/ [a panic?]" or as "and the belling of a stag grows in her fearful heart."[12] In the latter case the implication would be that the mating cry of the stag has made an indelible emotional impact on the hind and continues to influence her long after she has heard it. In either case the hind and the stag of the figure would symbolize, respectively, the wretched woman and her lover. And even if we follow Lobel and assign the heart to a serpent terrified by the belling of a stag,[13] the serpent would still represent the wretched woman, though the stag would now have to symbolize an assailant of some kind rather than a lover.

If, on the other hand, the deer is female, there are two possible explications. One is expressed in the translation "and a cry grows in the fearful heart of the hind," and according to it the hind would represent the wretched speaker; the cry, the speaker's terror. By the other explication, the translation would be "and the cry of a hind grows in my fearful heart," the heart belonging nonfiguratively to the woman speaking and "the cry of the hind" representing an emotion felt by this woman.

The above survey of interpretations, if one grants that Alcaeus's deer image must be either a simile or a metaphor, summarizes what is expressed or implied in current exegesis of the image. I myself see the logic in each of these explications, yet am somewhat uneasy with all of them. I would, therefore, like to indulge in some speculation of my own and to offer an exegesis of this image that impresses me as properly sensitive to Greek poetic usage at this early period as well as to what is known about the word *bromos*.

The deer (whether stag, hind, or fawn) is exceedingly common in Homeric similes, and almost invariably it appears as the prey of some other animal.[14] More often than not the other animal is a lion, as for instance at *Iliad* XI, lines 113-21:

> And as a lion seizes the innocent young of
>   the running
> deer, and easily crunches and breaks them
>   caught in the strong teeth
> when he has invaded their lair, and rips
>   out the soft heart from them,
> and even if the doe be very near, still
>   she has no strength
> to help, for the ghastly shivers of fear
>   are upon her also
> and suddenly she dashes away through the
>   glades and the timber
> sweating in her speed away from the pounce
>   of the strong beast;
> so there was no one of the Trojans who
>   could save these two
> from death, but they themselves were
>   running in fear from the Argives.[15]

I would suggest that this simile is instructive for the explication of Alcaeus's deer image. Also instructive is an occurrence of *bromos* in Euripides's *Heracles* (lines 1210-13). There, in an implied metaphor by which Heracles's rage is represented as that of a wild lion, *bromos* designates Heracles's murderous cry— if you will, his "roar."[16] Arrowsmith's translation, although it disguises the fact that *bromos* is a noun, nevertheless reproduces both the tone and the complexity of the Euripidean figure (Amphitryon is addressing Heracles): "O my son . . . / . . . tame that lion of your rage/ that roars you on to death."[17]

Taking the Homeric simile and this use of *bromos* in the *Heracles* as a point of perspective, I would suggest that Alcaeus's deer image was part of a simile in which the speaker of the lament compared herself to a hind terrified by the roar of a lion. The fearful heart would, therefore, belong to the hind, and the word for lion would have occurred in line 5. The following prose translation indicates, should my suggestion be correct, what would be the relation among the references to the deer, the roar, and the fearful heart: "And the roar [of the lion] causes [terror] to grow in the fearful heart of the hind." "Lady of Misery" (A 10) is too badly preserved to allow us to determine where the simile either began or ended, or how many verses it consumed. (Its beginning could have been at any point after the first verse, since any succeeding words and phrases are as appropriate to the simile as to the real situation.) Nor is there any evidence as to the source of the speaker's misery.[18] The notion that she is complaining of unrequited love is no more than a romantic and fanciful obeisance to modern taste.

The simile of "The Harlot" (F 3 [b], lines 26-27), though Homeric in vocabulary and style, is earthy in content: "giving something to a harlot/ is like throwing it into a wave of the surging salt sea." Equally Homeric in tone are the metaphorical designations of the sea turtle as "child of rock and surging sea" (Z 36) and of men as walls and cities (Z 103) or as "a city's martial rampart" (E 1, line 10).[19] Distinctively Alcaean, however, are the following metaphors: "wine's a window opening into a man" (Z 9), "day's a finger" ("Let Us Drink" = Z 22, line 1; used to indicate that it is twilight), and "the gates of spring are open" (P 2 [b], line 3).

CHAPTER 6

Myth, Legend, and Hymn

ALCAEUS draws from Greek mythology for three distinct purposes: to adorn his verses with incidental mythological references that have a stylistic and cosmetic function, to provide a major narrative for all or part of a given poem, and to acquire subject matter for hymns to various deities. I will examine Alcaeus's mythological references under these headings.

I Incidental References

We may classify as incidental the reference to Dionysus in "Let Us Drink" (Z 22): "Wine's the duller-of-grief the son of Zeus and Semele/ gave to men" (lines 3-4). The reference to Dionysus and the very fact that he is designated as "the son of Zeus and Semele" rather than simply as Dionysus enhances the stylistic level of a poem that is otherwise little more than a vigorous exhortation to heavy drinking. Alcaeus could have said straightforwardly that wine dulls grief; instead, he chose to give his poem an epic flavor by inserting a reference to Dionysus as "the son of Zeus and Semele." An epic flavor is also conveyed by the mention of "some Olympian" in the last stanza of "Pittacus" (D 12): "Let us cease from spirit-gnawing strife/ and fighting with kin, which some Olympian/ aroused, leading the people into folly/ and to Pittacus giving glory fair." Again, it is primarily a matter of poetic style that leads Alcaeus to refer to dying as either crossing "swirling Acheron" ("Sisyphus" = B 6 A, lines 2-3 and 8) or as entering "the house of Hades" (B 16, line 15). And if Page's translation of Z 57 is accurate ("I fell by the arts of the Cyprian goddess . . . "),[1] another example of mythological ornamentation is furnished by this one line fragment.

II Narratives

On the basis of the preserved fragments, the story of Troy was Alcaeus's favorite source for extended mythological narrative.

I have entitled B 10 "The Fall of Troy," since the poem begins
and ends with a reference to the destruction of Troy.[2] Despite
the mutilated state of this poem, it is possible to outline its content with considerable accuracy. Its opening stanza mentions
the destruction of "holy Ilium" and the miseries that befell
Priam and his sons "from you" (lines 1-4). The "from you"
indicates that some mythological person must have been
addressed with a vocative in this stanza, although the vocative
itself has not been preserved. The person so addressed may
have been Achilles, since he certainly was responsible for bringing misery to Priam and his sons and since his birth is recounted
in the last two stanzas (lines 12-14). Another possibility is Helen,
since she too is mentioned in the last stanza (line 15) and may
also be held responsible for bringing misery to Troy. In support
of taking Helen as the person addressed in the first stanza is the
fact that the second stanza opens with a reference to Achilles's
mother Thetis as being "different" (line 5). Different from
whom? The answer is obvious, if Helen was addressed in Stanza
1. I omit Paris from consideration; for, although he can be held
responsible for bringing misery to his native city, there is no
evidence that he is mentioned elsewhere in the poem.

So much for the opening of "The Fall of Troy" (B 10). The
narrative proper begins with the second stanza and tells both
of the marriage of Peleus and Thetis (lines 5-11) and of the
birth of their son Achilles (lines 12-14). The poem ends with
a terse couplet fraught with pathos: "But they [the Trojans]
perished for Helen/ together with their city." Such is the full
outline of "The Fall of Troy" (B 10). The narrative is brief
and allusive, and the poem's success depends on the final couplet
and on Alcaeus's use of a series of phrases pregnant with epic
connotation: "holy Ilium" (line 4), "graceful maiden" (line 8,
in reference to Thetis), "he loosed the maiden's girdle" (lines
9-10, indicating that Peleus and Thetis consummated their
marriage), and "happy driver of bay steeds" (line 14, descriptive
of Achilles.

In the case of "The Fall of Troy" (B 10), we were dealing
with a poem whose beginning and end were extant and whose
general content could be fully outlined. Both the beginning
and the end of "Helen" (N 1), however, are missing, so that it
is impossible to determine how much of the poem has been lost.
What remains tells the story of Helen: that she deserted her hus-

band and child to follow Paris to Troy (lines 3-10) and that because of her the Trojan plain was filled with destruction and slaughter (lines 12-17). True to his calling as a poet, Alcaeus is more concerned with scene and atmosphere than with straight narrative, for fully half of the remaining verses are devoted to a description of the havoc on the plain of Troy.

Achilles played a part in two other poems, "The Intercession" (B 12) and Z 31.[3] I follow Page in regarding the former, which is only eight verses in length, as a brief account of Thetis's intercession with Zeus on behalf of her son Achilles. The *Iliad* account of this event is quite elaborate and consumes 115 verses (Book I, lines 348-427 and 495-530), so that Alcaeus's poem must have been highly allusive, assuming a knowledge of the fuller Homeric account on the part of the reader. Not enough of Alcaeus's poem remains to permit a critical evaluation of it. Even scantier are the remains of Z 31 (only five words in Greek): "Achilles, lord of the Scythian land." The reference to Scythia, however, reveals that Alcaeus was at least familiar with the legend according to which Achilles was transported after death to the White Island near the mouths of the Danube, where he lived as Lord of Pontos or, as here in Z 31, as "lord of the Scythian land."

There are still further vestiges of Alcaeus's narration of the myths and legends associated with the Trojan War and the return to Greece of the Achaean warriors. The mighty Telamonian Ajax figured in at least one of Alcaeus's poems, for he is described in the single verse of Z 64 as "descendant of the royal son of Cronus, Ajax, second only to Achilles in valor." And we learn from Z 118 that the Phaeacians, the gracious and fabulous hosts of Odysseus in the *Odyssey*, were, according to Alcaeus, "sprung from the blood drops of Uranus." The sin and punishment of Ajax the Locrian were rather fully narrated in "Ajax and Cassandra" (Q 1), a comparatively long poem whose beginning and end are missing but which is represented by forty-nine partially preserved verses.[4] It is clear from what survives that Alcaeus narrated that Ajax violated Cassandra during the sacking of Troy, even though she sought sanctuary at the image of Athena, and that the goddess as punishment shattered the entire fleet of the Achaeans as they attempted to return home from Troy. Such phrases as "Athena loaded with booty" (line 9) and "over the wine-dark sea" (lines 25-26) give the narrative an epic tone. Alcaeus, however, must have in some manner connected his epic narrative with contemporary politics; for, although the bulk of line 47 is missing, enough survives to reveal a reference to Alcaeus's political archenemy Pittacus. Perhaps Alcaeus issued a warning that, just as Ajax the Locrian caused the destruction of the Achaean fleet, so might Pittacus the son of Hyrrhas bring to ruin the entire polis of Mytilene.

Alcaeus's use of non-Trojan myth and legend for narrative reasons is attested by several brief fragments. According to Z 120, Alcaeus assigned nine heads to the Hydra; it is, therefore, likely that Alcaeus narrated the tale of Heracles's conquest of this monster. Also, the opening words of the Alcaean fragment numbered 317 in Lobel and Page's edition bear a striking resemblance to Hesiod's statement that Zeus gave Endymion permission to choose the time of his own death.[5] It is, therefore, highly possible both that Alcaeus employed an extended Endymion narrative and that he used Hesiod as his source of information. The Alcaean fragment, however, is so corrupt as to rule out certainty. The circumstances are similar in the case of M 4, where one of the fragment's few complete words is *kibisin* (accusative case of *kibisis*), a rare word used especially of the pouch in which Perseus carried the severed head of Medusa.[6] Again, though only speculation is permissible, it may be that in M 4 Alcaeus narrated at some length the tale of Perseus's slaying of Medusa.

Two longer though mutilated poems also attest to Alcaeus's use of non-Trojan myth and legend for narratives. We may speculate with some confidence that A 7 told the story of Phalanthus, the traditional founder of Tarentum in southern Italy: Phalanthus was shipwrecked in the sea of Crisa on his way to Italy and was carried safely to land by a dophin.[7] The evidence for such speculation may be summarized as follows. A 7 contains vocabulary appropriate to a sea voyage as well as references to Crisa and a fish; in addition, the first three letters in the name Phalanthus occur at the end of the extant part of verse 11, right before it breaks off. It appears, therefore, that Alcaeus was narrating the same legend of which Pausanias speaks (X, 13, 10): "They say that before he reached Italy Phalanthus was shipwrecked in the sea of Crisa and was carried safely to land by a dolphin."

The other longer fragment is "Sisyphus" (B 6 A). In the first verse Alcaeus exhorts his comrade Melanippus to "drink . . . with me," and there follow morbid references to the inevitability of death that are not entirely decipherable (lines 2-4). Then Alcaeus turns to the story of Sisyphus (lines 5-10), who was the shrewdest of men and once even escaped from death, but who eventually died and was punished by Zeus in Hades. The Sisyphus narrative functions as a mythological exemplum: if even Sisyphus, the shrewdest of men, was subject to death, how much more certain is death for us ordinary mortals. This being the case, let us drink and enjoy life while we can, Melanippus! Sisyphus is again mentioned in the last verse of "The Harlot" (F 3 [b]), but so little of the surrounding context has survived that it is impossible to tell whether the mention is incidental or is part of a fuller narrative.

III *The Hymns*

The hymn was one of Alcaeus's favorite poetic forms; and it is certain that he wrote hymns in honor of Apollo, Hermes, Hephaestus, the Dioscuri, Athena, Eros, and the river Hebrus.[8] There is also evidence for hymns to Artemis, Demeter, and, possibly, even Poseidon and the Nymphs. The thirty-three hymns of varying length and to various deities that have come down as part of the Homeric corpus attest to the extensive popularity of this particular literary form during the era in which Alcaeus lived and wrote. The Alcaean and the Homeric Hymns resemble one another in two general features. Both take as their themes the achievements, adventures, and attributes of the deity to whom they are addressed; and both are literary endeavors rather than devotional pieces designed for presentation at cult ceremonies. After this, the resemblance diminishes rapidly, and there is little (and no sure) evidence that Alcaeus ever drew his subject matter directly from a Homeric hymn. In fact, in those instances when Alcaeus and the Homeric Rhapsode have a common subject, as in the case of their hymns to Apollo (Homeric Hymn 3, entry 307 in Lobel and Page's edition of Alcaeus), Hermes (Homeric Hymn 4, entry 308 in Lobel and Page's edition of Alcaeus), and the Dioscuri (Homeric Hymn 33, B 2 [a] in the Alcaean corpus), the discrepancies between the corresponding hymns are in general far more striking than the similarities.

Alcaeus's Hymn to Apollo has derived nothing from the Delian part of the Homeric Hymn; and, although Alcaeus's poem covers the same general events narrated in the Delphian part of the Homeric Hymn, the details of these events differ greatly from poem to poem. For example, both Alcaeus and the Rhapsode bring Apollo to Delphi from the north; yet in Alcaeus's hymn the journey starts from the land of the Hyperboreans and is made by air in a chariot drawn by swans, while the Rhapsode brings Apollo to Delphi from Olympus by land. Again, Alcaeus's Hymn to Hermes tells of Hermes's theft of Apollo's quiver, an episode not mentioned in the corresponding Homeric Hymn. And, finally, the focal point of Alcaeus's "Castor and Polydeuces" is the manifestation of the Dioscuri as saviors in the form of Saint Elmo's fire, a point which receives only a three-word allusion in the Homeric Hymn (line 12). Let us now examine Alcaeus's hymns in more detail.

Our knowledge of the Hymn to Apollo is quite full. Although only portions of two separate verses are preserved, there are references to its content by Plutarch and by Pausanias; and the sophistic orator Himerius has left a rather detailed summary of the events narrated in the Hymn, or a least of a substantial portion of these events.[9] We know that the Hymn began with the vocative phrases "Oh lord Apollo, son of great Zeus . . . " and that in its introduction Alcaeus described Castalia's water as a gift of the Cephisus (the Castalian spring and the Cephisus River are both located in the vicinity of Delphi). It is likely that the phrase "joy of Tritaea" (Tritaea is a village near Delphi), which Alcaeus too applied to the Castalian spring, also occurred in the introduction of the Hymn. We are, therefore, certain that the Hymn opened with an invocation of Apollo and that this invocation was followed by introductory references to certain natural features of the area around Delphi. These references are entirely in keeping with the narrative content of the Hymn; for, as we shall see from Himerius's summary, Delphi was Apollo's ultimate and ordained destination, and one of the Hymn's aesthetic highlights was a description of the joyous reception Apollo received when he finally reached Delphi.

Himerius informs us that Alcaeus told the following story about Apollo in this Hymn. When Apollo was born, Zeus gave him a golden diadem, a lyre, and a chariot drawn by swans and then dispatched him to Delphi and the streams of Castalia.

Apollo's ordained mission was to expound justice and right (*dikē* and *themis*) to the Hellenes. Instead of following his father's instruction, however, Apollo drove his chariot to the land of the Hyperboreans. When the Delphians discovered this, they composed a paean in honor of Apollo and had youths sing and dance about his tripod, trying to persuade him to leave the Hyperboreans and come to them. Nevertheless, Apollo spent a full year proclaiming laws to the Hyperboreans, and only when he had decided it was time for the tripods at Delphi to sound forth did he command his swans to fly there. Alcaeus brought Apollo to Delphi at midsummer, and all nature responded to the god's arrival. His lyre sprouted shoots of green, and nightingales sang as beautifully as birds are wont to sing in the poems of Alcaeus. The swallows and cicadas ceased lamenting their own misfortunes among men, and all their strains were sung in honor of the god. In the spirit of poetry, Castalia gushed forth with silver waters, and great Cephisus rose up with surging waves; for Alcaeus is compelled like Homer to make even water capable of sensing the presence of deity.

Such is Himerius's summary. The only additional detail about this Hymn comes from the pseudo-Plutarchan *De Musica* (1135 F — 1136 A), which informs us that the dancing and rites in honor of Apollo were accompanied by flute music. Himerius's summary, as I take it, indicates that the song of the nightingales was portrayed, by whatever poetic devices, with great beauty and sensitivity and, furthermore, that in describing the reaction of the Castalian spring and the Cephisus to Apollo's presence Alcaeus was overwhelmed with poetic inspiration. It is clear from all this that in this Hymn Alcaeus is ever the poet, using his narrative as a framework to which he attaches images designed to captivate the reader's sense of sight and sound.

About the Hymn to Hermes much less is known.[10] Alcaeus, we are informed by one ancient witness, wrote a hymn in honor of this deity's birth and childhood; and Pausanias (VII, 20, 4) mentions an episode that occurred in Alcaeus's "hymn to Hermes." It is reasonable to assume that both witnesses are referring to the same work and that the following verses constituted the opening of the Hymn (Hermes was born on Mount Cyllene and was the son of Zeus and Maia): "Hail, thou ruler of Cyllene, since 'tis my/ intent to hymn, whom on the peaks . . . / Maia bore, having lain with Cronus's son/ the almighty. . . ."[11]

In addition, we learn from Pausanias (VII, 20, 4) and from Horace's imitation of this Hymn (*Odes* I, 10, lines 9-12) that Alcaeus told how Hermes as a boy stole Apollo's cattle. It is also likely that Alcaeus included a humorous touch: while Apollo was upbraiding Hermes for stealing his cattle, the mischievous young god managed in some way to accomplish the theft of Apollo's quiver, at which the older god could not refrain from laughing.[12] Finally, we learn from Z 124 that Alcaeus somewhere introduces Hermes as the Cupbearer of the gods. It may well be that it was in the Hymn to Hermes, since the Hymn told of the god's boyhood and since youthful beauty was a standard attribute for the office of Cupbearer.[13]

The extant information about this Hymn indicates that in it Alcaeus maintained a mood quite different from that of the Hymn to Apollo with its high pageantry and brilliant images. Apollo's divinely ordained mission to establish an oracular shrine at Delphi and to expound *dikē* and *themis* to all the Hellenes demanded a mood more stately than that suitable to the escapades of a mischievous young god. The Hymn to Hermes was accordingly a lighter, more playful set of verses.

The Hymn to Hephaestus is represented by even scantier remains, and some speculation is involved in reconstructing its content.[14] Our point of reference in this task will be a late account of Hephaestus's expulsion from and restoration to heaven that is consistent with the account of these matters given in the eighteenth book of the *Iliad*, lines 394-405 (the account in Book I, lines 590-94 is quite different and need not concern us here). According to our late authority, Hera expelled Hephaestus from heaven because she was ashamed of his lameness. He proceeded to master the artisan's craft and, in revenge, manufactured a chair with invisible chains, which he sent to his mother as a gift. She was delighted with the present, sat down in it, and was of course bound fast. Since no one else was able to free her, the gods deliberated as to how they might persuade Hephaestus to return and release his mother. Ares undertook to bring him back but returned in disgrace, having been frightened away by Hephaestus's firebrands. Hera was now in extreme distress and was saved only by Dionysus, who got Hephaestus drunk and thereby enticed him to return and free Hera. In recompense and gratitude to Dionysus for this service, Hera persuaded the other Olympians to accept him, though a latecomer, as one of their number.

This is a summary of the fullest version available of a story prominent in Greek literature and vase paintings.[15] Although the author of the summary nowhere mentions the name of Alcaeus, it is my belief that the story just summarized gives the narrative substance of Alcaeus's Hymn to Hephaestus. The justification for such an interpretation is that all possible fragments of the Hymn are at least consistent with the narrative just given. This is not to claim, however, that Alcaeus told the story in the same detail that is present in the version summarized. Indeed, to judge from the narrative technique employed in "The Fall of Troy" (B 10), "Helen" (N 1), "The Intercession" (B 12), "Ajax and Cassandra" (Q 1), and "Sisyphus" (B 6 A), Alcaeus assumed on his readers' part a general knowledge of the Hephaestus story and singled out for emphasis only those elements that especially suited his poetic intent. Much of Alcaeus's narrative would have been brief and allusive.

The evidence for connecting the above story of Hephaestus's revenge on Hera with Alcaeus's Hymn to Hephaestus is as follows. From Z 25 we learn that Alcaeus composed a hymn celebrating the birth and childhood of Hephaestus. The events summarized above would suit such a hymn, since they occurred soon after the birth of Hephaestus.[16] Of the fragments listed by Lobel and Page under Z 25, the first is expressly attributed to Alcaeus by our ancient source and is thoroughly in harmony with the above prose summary: "so that none of the Olympians/ could free [her] without him ... " According to the proposed interpretation, the "him" would be Hephaestus and the supplied "her" his mother Hera. The second Z 25 fragment has been assigned in modern times to Alcaeus with good reason but not with certainty:[17] "and Ares says that he will bring Hephaestus by force." If actually by Alcaeus, these words are strikingly suitable to the story that I believe Alcaeus was narrating in his Hymn to Hephaestus. The third Z 25 fragment was attributed to Alcaeus in antiquity and has been assigned to the Hymn to Hephaestus by a number of modern editors: "one of the twelve."[18] Such a phrase would be appropriate in a Hymn which told of Dionysus's enrollment among the Olympians. The fact that Dionysus was actually the thirteenth Olympian need cause no difficulty, since "the twelve" is no more than a synonym for "the Olympians."[19]

Another fragment assigned to the Hymn to Hephaestus by some editors is "and the immortal gods laughed."[20] This assignment is the hardest to justify, since we are as unsure of its authorship as we are of the poem to which it belongs. The case for assigning it to the Hymn to Hephaestus rests solely on two facts: twice in Homer the gods laughed at Hephaestus (Iliad I, lines 599-600 and Odyssey VIII, lines 326-27), and the drunken Hephaestus of the Hymn would be a fit cause for laughter on Olympus. This is pushing speculation to the extreme!

Any assessment of the mood of this Hymn is fraught with uncertainty. Nevertheless, some cautious speculation seems to be in order. If Alcaeus did in fact introduce a drunken Hephaestus, it is likely that he was in the Hymn to Hephaestus striving for a comic mood, one in the spirit of Odyssey VIII, lines 266-366. There it is told how Hephaestus manufactured invisible chains, with which he entrapped Ares and Aphrodite in the very act of adulterous love, and how the male divinities came to laugh at the plight of the hapless pair. Such a mood would be quite different from either the exalted one of the Hymn to Apollo or the playful one of the Hymn to Hermes.

The attribution of a Hymn to Artemis to Alcaeus rests on very slight evidence. A fragment of such a piece (T 1 in Lobel and Page's edition), written in the same Lesbian Aeolic in which Alcaeus wrote, has been preserved; but there is no indication of the author's name. The only basis for assigning the poem to Alcaeus is our knowledge that the hymn was one of his favorite poetic forms. The opening of the poem is missing, and the extant phrases indicate that the author is describing Artemis's oath of perpetual virginity. Beyond this, nothing can reasonably be said about the poem.

We have what is for Alcaeus a rather full text and are, therefore, on much surer grounds when we turn to "Castor and Polydeuces" (B 2 [a]), a Hymn to the Dioscuri, the traditional saviors of storm-tossed mariners. Since this Hymn has already been examined in some detail for evidence of allegory, I will omit allegorical considerations from the present discussion. The poem is clearly a hymn, for it opens (lines 1-4) with an invocation of the Dioscuri, in which they are addressed in the vocative as Castor and Polydeuces, designated as sons of Zeus and Leda, and urgently enjoined to manifest themselves. The injunction "manifest yourselves" (line 3) can only mean that Alcaeus is depicting himself as actually on board a storm-racked ship desperately in need of help from the Dioscuri. The second stanza of the Hymn (lines 5-8) is complete. It describes the Dioscuri as those "who over broad earth and the sea/ entire do go on steeds swift-footed/ and easily men do save from death/ so chilling." The third stanza (lines 9-12), which is marred by the loss of several words, tells how the saviors manifest themselves as Saint Elmo's fire ("and in troublous night bringing light/ to a dark ship"). The rest of the Hymn is lost. In it Alcaeus must have described the plight of his own vessel and explained his immediate need.

What is unusual about this Hymn is that it is presented in the vivid present and functions simultaneously as a tribute to its honorees and as an urgent appeal for their help. It is permeated by a mood of present urgency and in this respect differs from Alcaeus's other Hymns. In this same respect it bears two striking similarities to Sappho's famous Hymn to Aphrodite.[21] Sappho's poem also opens with an urgent appeal to its recipient for help (lines 1-4), in which Aphrodite is addressed in the vocative and is designated as "daughter of Zeus." (This mood of present urgency is reinforced in the last stanza, which begins "Come to me now!" Whether or not Alcaeus introduced such a renewal of appeal near the end of the Hymn to the Dioscuri is beyond our knowledge, since the whole latter part of his poem has been lost.) And just as Alcaeus's Hymn turns immediately after stanza 1 to a description of the customary, beneficent activities of the Dioscuri, so at the same point in its structure does Sappho's Hymn turn to a description of the benefits she has customarily received from Aphrodite. Beyond these two points, there is no basis for comparison, since Alcaeus's Hymn breaks off in the midst of the description just mentioned. It may be, however, that in the case of these two poems we are dealing with a type of hymn especially cultivated by Aeolic poets of the era of Sappho and Alcaeus.

The Hymn to Athena and the Hymn to Eros may be placed in a special category and treated together. As far as we can tell, their basic type and nature does not differ substantively from those of the Hymns to Apollo, Hermes, and Hephaestus. What sets the Hymns to Athena and to Eros apart is that their subjects are deities of local cult rather than pan-Hellenic divinities, as are the subjects of the hymns just mentioned.[22]

The single preserved fragment of the Hymn to Athena (Z 1) consists of four verses too badly damaged to allow us to analyze its syntax. Nevertheless, its first two words, a vocative address to "Queen Athena," are extant; and it is certain that the Athena of this hymn is the one who carries the cognomen Itonia; that is, she is a local and not the pan-Hellenic Athena. The geographer Strabo is the source of the single fragment of this Hymn (IX, 2, 29). Immediately before quoting Alcaeus, he writes that after the Trojan War the Boeotians founded in the plain before the city of Coronea a temple for the Itonian Athena and that Cuarius was the name they gave to the nearby river. The Alcaean quotation is introduced by Strabo to demonstrate that Alcaeus called this river Coralius rather than Cuarius. The Alcaean fragment mentions "Coronea" and contains the phrases "in front of the temple" and "beside the banks of the Coralius river." The information from Strabo and the remains of the quotations neatly complement one another: the conclusion is demanded that Alcaeus's Hymn celebrated Athena Itonia, a local Boeotian goddess.

A similar conclusion is appropriate to the Hymn to Eros (Z 3). Eros was a deity distinguished for the absence of shrines and formal rites in his honor, and of the few cults devoted to him during the period of Alcaeus the most famous was at Thespiae in Boeotia.[23] It is, therefore, a priori likely that a Hymn to Eros would be to a local rather than to a pan-Hellenic deity. Furthermore, since in the Hymn to Athena Itonia, Alcaeus demonstrated an interest in a particular Boeotian cult and since the most famous cult of Eros during Alcaeus's lifetime was at Thespiae in Boeotia, the conclusion is justified that the Eros of Alcaeus's Hymn was the Eros worshiped locally at Thespiae. The preserved fragment (Z 3) is brief but nearly perfect, as far as it goes. It must derive from the beginning of the Hymn, for Eros is addressed (I translate the entire fragment) as "most terrible of gods,/ whom fair-sandled Iris bore,/ having lain with Zephyr of the golden hair." The phrase translated as "most terrible of the gods" (*deinotaton* [accusative] *theōn*) could also bear the rendering "most clever of gods." Only the succeeding context, which is lost beyond recovery, could furnish evidence sufficient to dictate one or the other translation. The brilliant and connotative parentage here ascribed to Eros (Iris, the Rainbow, for his mother; Zephyr, the West Wind, for his father) may be peculiar to the cult god of Thespiae.[24] Again, it may be the creation of Alcaeus's poetic imagination.

The remains, both real and speculative, of Alcaeus's Hymns indicate that the hymn was a poetic form in which he excelled. He himself must have sensed this fact; otherwise he would not have chosen to compose in it so frequently. These facts make it all the more regrettable that so much of Alcaeus's hymnal poetry has perished. In addition to the fragments already examined, there remain only a few, small bits that may have come from other hymns. The isolated half-verse mentioning "your daughter" (*tea kora*) and her admiration for some deed (item 310 in Lobel and Page's edition) would suit a Hymn to Demeter, for the Homeric hymn to this same goddess (number 2) told of Demeter's search for her daughter Kore, who had been carried off by Hades. Also, this half-verse is ascribed by its source to the first book of Alcaeus's poems, and we know that in the Alexandrian edition this first book opened with the Hymns to Apollo and to Hermes.[25] There is, finally, a possibility that such fragments as Z 10 ("not yet had Poseidon/ struck the briny sea . . .") and Z 19 (a reference to the Nymphs being the daughters of aegis-bearing Zeus) occurred in hymns to divinities. Indeed, a hymnal classification for Z 19 is strongly recommended by evidence that did not come to light until 1968, more than a decade after the publication of Lobel and Page's monumental edition of the Sapphic and Alcaean corpus. This evidence is in the form of a papyrus fragment (number 2734, Fragment 1 in the Oxyrhynchus collection) which is well enough preserved to reveal that it contained successive summaries of the Hymn to Apollo, the Hymn to Hermes, and of Z 19.[26] The papyrus, furthermore, seems to indicate that the single preserved verse of Z 19 is this poem's beginning and that the poem stood third in the Alexandrian edition of Alcaeus's works. Since this edition opened wth the two hymns just mentioned, we may reasonably, though cautiously, classify the third poem as also a hymn, especially since it begins with a verse appropriate to a Hymn to the Nymphs.[27]

There remains for consideration one poem that defies general classification and that is admittedly out of place in a chapter dealing primarily with the poetic uses of myth. It is in the form of a hymn; but, as far as can be judged from its surviving portion, it is devoid of any mythological element, unless the personification and possible apotheosis of a river be regarded as a mythological feature. The Hebrus runs through central Thrace and debouches into the Aegean near Aenus. The Hymn to the Hebrus (B 13) opens with the couplet, "Hebrus, fairest of rivers are you as by Aenus/ you pour forth into the surging sea," and is represented by two stanzas that are only partially damaged. In hymnal style, the opening address to the Hebrus in the vocative is followed by a description of the river's activities: you surge through the land of Thrace (lines 2-4), and many maidens bathe in your waters (lines 5-8). In the second stanza are beguiling yet syntactically enigmatic references to the thighs and soft hands of the maidens, to some (apparently the girls) who are "charmed," and to the river's "divine water." To judge from what remains of this hymn, it was, from the perspective of vivid yet controlled imagery, one of Alcaeus's finest poetic achievements.

CHAPTER 7

Literary Influence
and Poetic Environment

IN this chapter I propose to relate Alcaeus's poetry to the
antecedent and contemporary poetic traditions by which he
was obviously inspired or to which he may reasonably be
believed to have reacted. Such a task is a legitimate critical
enterprise, providing it does not delude either reader or critic
into the fallacy of thinking that this is the study of poetry proper.
What it is, is the study of the means whereby poets are molded
and poetry is endowed with subject matter and style. There is
a sure difference between the study of a poem as an independent
literary entity and the study of its sources of inspiration, whether
they be stylistic or substantive. At the same time, the study of
literary influence affecting a given body of poetry, when prac-
ticed with discretion and with perspective, is both critically
functional and psychologically expedient: it enhances our
capacity for establishing rapport with that poetry as well as our
ability to subject it to critical explanation.

I The Epic Influence

The epic influence on Alcaeus is clear and definable and may
be analyzed under the headings of (1) subject matter and (2)
diction and style. For convenience I will include within the *epic*
rubric only the *Iliad* and the *Odyssey*, which may be designated
conjointly as *Homer,* and the poems of the post-Homeric Epic
Cycle, all of which deal in some way with the Trojan War or
its aftermath.[1] The term epic could, of course, encompass in
addition both Hesiod and the Homeric Hymns. The traces of
Hesiodic influence on Alcaeus, however, are of a special sort and
will be examined separately; and the Homeric Hymns may be
disposed of with the observations that they share with Alcaeus's
hymns only certain exterior features due to a common literary

form and that whatever influence on Alcaeus's style or diction
might conceivably be postulated must have emanated originally
from the Homeric epics themselves. The evidence argues that
Alcaeus never drew the substance of any of his hymns directly
from a Homeric Hymn.[2] In conclusion, two points should be
stressed. The epic meter, the dactylic hexameter, is excluded
from immediate purview, for even when borrowing epic subject matter or imitating epic style Alcaeus continued to compose
in the meters peculiar to his own dialect. Also, I have so con-
structed my critical methodology at this point as to avoid becoming embroiled in problems occasioned by the oral composition of the Homeric poems. I realize, of course, that Alcaeus
may have encountered the *Iliad* and the *Odyssey* in versions
somewhat different from those known to us.[3]

We may begin our examination of Alcaeus's use of epic subject matter by glancing at Z 64, a single verse preserved without
any indication of its context, and Z 118, a brief remark by a
scholiast. The former describes Telamonian Ajax as "descendant
of the royal son of Cronus, Ajax, second only to Achilles in
valor," and in the latter the scholiast informs us that the
Phaeacians were, according to Alcaeus, "sprung from the blood
drops of Uranus." The description of Ajax is reminiscent of *Iliad*
II (lines 768-69), *Iliad* XVII (lines 278-80), and *Odyssey* XI
(lines 469-70); Ajax is assigned a prominent role in the *Iliad;*
and the Phaeacians are Odysseus's hosts throughout Books VI-XII
of the *Odyssey.* Either or both of these fragments, therefore,
could derive from poems in which Alcaeus made extensive use
of Homeric subject matter. On the other hand, speculation is
idle: in neither instance are we informed of context, and the
Phaeacian reference calls to mind no particular *Odyssey* verses.

On the other hand, there are a series of poems that deal
with epic themes and give evidence of Alcaeus's continuing use
of epic subject matter. It is noteworthy, however, that Alcaeus
never tells the full epic story; he only summarizes or refers to
it in such a way as to indicate he is presuming on his reader's
part a knowledge of a much fuller, epic version. Such is the
case with "The Fall of Troy" (B 10), a four-stanza poem of only
sixteen verses that either mentions or briefly narrates, in addition
to the destruction of the city itself, events that occurred long
before the Trojan War and served as a prelude to it. We
possess the beginning and the end of "The Fall of Troy" as

well as a substantial portion of each stanza, so that it is possible to outline the general content of the entire poem. After opening references to "holy Ilium" and to the miseries that befell Priam and his sons (lines 1-4), Alcaeus reverts over many years to the marriage of Achilles's parents, Peleus and Thetis, and devotes the next two stanzas to this event (lines 5-12). The last stanza offers two verses briefly narrating the birth of Achilles and ends with a two-verse reference to the fall of Troy: "But they [the Trojans] perished for Helen/ together with their city." The knowledge presumed by Alcaeus on the part of his reader is, basically, the full content of the *Iliad*.

A smilar presumption characterizes "Helen" (N 1), though here, since both the beginning and the end of the poem are missing, we cannot be sure of its length; nor can we know what details from the story of Troy were included in the lost portions. We can, however, reconstruct the general content of the poem's nineteen surviving or partially surviving verses: driven mad with love for Paris, Helen deserted her husband and her child to sail with him to Troy (lines 3-10); because of Helen, the Trojan plain was filled with slaughter and the wreckage of many chariots (lines 11-18). This reconstruction is extracted from four more or less decipherable stanzas of four verses each. Two of these stanzas narrate the story of Helen, the other two depict the carnage and destruction that occurred "because of that woman" (line 14). In "Helen," therefore, Alcaeus is at least as much interested in mood and atmosphere as he is in pure narration. And it is because of the universally common knowledge of the *Iliad* in the Greek world that it is both possible and reasonable for him to sacrifice narrative detail to mood and atmosphere.

Were it not for this common knowledge of Homer by Alcaeus's audience, such a poem as "The Intercession" (B 12) would not have been artistically feasible; for in this piece Alcaeus obviously presumes a knowledge of the first 530 lines of the *Iliad* and then narrates in not more than eight and possibly as few as four verses an event that consumed 115 of Homer's hexameters (*Iliad* I, lines 348-427 and 495-530). The first four verses of "The Intercession" are represented by only a few isolated letters, but enough of the last four verses has survived to reveal that they told of Achilles's appeal to his mother Thetis for help and of her intercession with Zeus on his behalf.[4] Since this poem is eight verses in total length, Alcaeus could have given only a minimum amount of narrative detail, even if the entire poem was devoted to only the appeal-intercession episode.

A comparison of Alcaeus's with the Homeric account of this episode will be useful for appreciating the manner and extent of the lyric poet's condensation of epic source material. The *Iliad* version is divided into two parts and runs as follows. In the first (lines 348-427), after Patroclus has led Briseis away, Achilles withdraws to the seashore where in tears he calls upon his mother and complains of the insult he has received from Agamemnon. Thetis hears his cry and rises like a mist from the sea to comfort him. After some hesitation, Achilles takes twenty-six verses (366-92) to tell his mother why Agamemnon has dishonored him by depriving him of his concubine Briseis. He then reminds her in full detail of a great favor she had in the past conferred on Zeus and asks her to go to Zeus on his behalf. The plea she is to convey to Zeus is that he will help the Trojans to drive the Achaeans with great losses back to their ships so that Agamemnon's folly will be exposed to his army and he himself will come to recognize the folly of provoking Achilles to retire from battle. Thetis in reply attempts to comfort her son and promises to carry out his request. In the second part of the *Iliad* account (lines 495-530), after intervening narrative covering other events, the epic poet returns to Thetis and describes her meeting with Zeus: Thetis puts the request; Zeus hesitates with the explanation that Hera will be angry if he grants it, but finally agrees. His assent is marked by an inviolable guarantee, the shaking of his head.

In comparison with "The Intercession" (B 12) with its brief and allusive use of detail in its last four verses (Achilles calls upon his mother, she pleads with Zeus for him), the *Iliad* account is surfeited with narrative matter. An even more striking feature of the epic version, however, is its dramatic nature. I am referring to its abundance of dialogue, with the bulk of its narrative matter assigned to the various *dramatis personae*—that is, to Achilles, Thetis, and Zeus. In fact, of the hundred and fifteen *Iliad* verses allotted to this episode, ninety are in the form of dialogue: strip the account of its dialogue, and there are only twenty-five verses left. This, I would suggest, is basically what Alcaeus has done—not only here but in "The Fall of Troy" (B 10) and "Helen" (N 1) as well, though in these latter two poems the facts of the matter are not so readily demonstrable. Alcaeus thus, when he borrows subject matter from Homer, discards its dialogue—that is, its dramatic trappings—and employs it to write poems that are truly narrative, as against the dramatic-narrative poetry of his source.

The absence of dialogue and the concentration on pure narrative are also apparent in "Ajax and Cassandra" (Q 1), the only other poem that reveals direct and extensive use of epic subject matter.[5] Interpretive limitations, however, are imposed by the poor condition of the verses preceding and following the better-preserved portion of the Ajax-Cassandra narrative. It is impossible to determine the length of the poem (parts, often meager parts, of forty-nine verses remain), and difficult to assess the function of the narrative within the poem as a whole. Though the narrative is extensive and probably formed the core of the poem, it undoubtedly served an ulterior purpose as well; for the survival of a patronymic for Pittacus in verse 47 reveals that Alcaeus must have established a connection between the Ajax-Cassandra episode and contemporary, Mytilenean politics. At any rate, the decipherable portion of "Ajax and Cassandra" (lines 4-27) is quick, concise narrative and may be summarized as follows. As the Achaeans sailed past Aegae on their return to Greece from Troy, they encountered a devastating storm, divinely sent as retribution for the sin of one man, Ajax the Locrian (not the great Telamonian Ajax previously mentioned). Ajax, Alcaeus continues, had violated Cassandra during the sacking of Troy as she sought refuge at the image of Athena, and in rage the goddess rushed over the wine-dark sea to stir up angry gales and wreck the returning fleet. We know that the story of this shipwreck (and presumably that of the violation of Cassandra) was told in the *Nostoi,* one of the poems of the Epic Cycle; and the shipwreck itself, together with details of Ajax's death and a passing allusion to the anger of Athena, is mentioned in the *Odyssey* (Book IV, lines 495-511). There is, however, no indication that Alcaeus was imitating or adapting these *Odyssey* verses, so that the most precise statement permissible regarding his source material is that it was epic.

In summary, Alcaeus draws freely from epic poetry for subject matter, but he in no way feels bound by the conventions of epic poetry and employs this epic material in his own manner to satisfy his own lyric interest. He rejects two basic features of

epic poetry, the dactylic hexameter and the dramatic use of
dialogue, the former in favor of his native Aeolic meters and the
latter in favor of a more purely narrative style. Also, he presumes
on the part of his audience a knowledge both of the fuller
epic version of each story he narrates and of the Homeric
poems in general. The result is a narrative that is restrained,
allusive, and pregnant with epic connotations.[6]

Let us now turn to the other area of epic influence on
Alcaeus's poetry, that of diction and style.[7] My goal here is not
to present a complete and comprehensive analysis, but through a
selection of representative categories of influence and, within
these categories, of illustrative examples to depict the type and
nature rather than the exact amount of Alcaeus's debt to his
epic heritage. I will first examine Alcaeus's use of noun-epithet
phrases that are either borrowed verbatim from Homer or are
closely modeled on Homeric formulas.[8] Such phrases characterize, but are by no means confined to, poems with mythological
and epic subject matter. In fact, they permeate Alcaeus's poetry
and serve to give it an elevated, Homeric tone that is as immediately apparent to the modern critic as it would have been
to an ancient reader.

There is a smooth blending of style with theme when noun-
epithet phrases occur in epic and mythological contexts. In "The
Fall of Troy" (B 10) we encounter "holy Ilium" (line 4) and
a description of Achilles as a driver "of bay steeds" (line 14).
"Holy" is applied to cities (it modifies "Ilium," for example, at
Iliad IV, line 46) throughout the Homeric poems; and "bay"
describes horses at *Iliad* IX, line 407 and XI, line 680. Again, in
"Helen" (N 1) Alcaeus assigns Helen the commonest of her
Homeric epithets, "Argive" (line 4), and introduces in verse 16
"quick-eyed," one of Homer's most frequent epithets. "Castor
and Polydeuces" (B 2) exhibits a profusion of this sort of noun-
epithet combination. Straight out of Homer are "broad earth"
(line 5), "swift-footed steeds" (line 6), "well-benched ships"
(line 9), and "dark ship" (line 12); and the addition of Alcaeus's
own Homeric variations "chilling death" (lines 7-8) and "troublous night" (line 11) serves to intensify the carefully devised
epic tone of this poem. And mythological subject matter offers
Alcaeus the opportunity for several other noteworthy noun-
epithet phrases of a strikingly epic tone: in "Sisyphus" (B 6 A),
"swirling Acheron" (twice, in lines 2 and 8), and "dark earth";

in the Hymn to Eros (Z 3), "fair-sandled Iris" and "golden-haired Zephyr"; in Z 10, "briny sea"; in Z 19, "aegis-bearing Zeus"; and, finally, in "Ajax and Cassandra" (Q 1), "Athena loaded with booty" (line 9) and "wine-dark sea" (lines 25-26).

The employ of such noun-epithet phrases, as has already been observed, is not confined to mythological and Homeric themes. 'The Prayer" (G 1) offers "bright precinct" (line 2), "blessed immortals" (line 4), and "glorious goddess" (line 6). Even more emphatic are the "blessed gods" (line 28), "dark earth" (line 29), "maidens of Lesbos in trailing robes" (lines 32-33), and "divine sound" (line 34) of "Exile" (G 2). Verbatim repetitions of Homeric phrases are afforded by the "hoary sea" of Z 36, by the "long-winged birds" of "Wild Ducks" (Z 21), by the reference to "a wave of the hoary sea" in "The Harlot" (line 27; F 3 [b]), and by the "dark ship" in verse 4 of one of the nautical allegories ("The Ship: II" = Z 2); and Alcaeus's "spirit-devouring sedition" (*thymoboros lya*) at verse 10 of "Pittacus" (D 12) is reminiscent of Homer's recurrent "spirit-devouring strife" (*thymoboros eris*). In addition, an epic tone is imparted by "holy Babylon" in B 16, line 10 and by the "surging sea" at verse 2 of the Hymn to the Hebrus (B 13).

We have been examining Alcaeus's artistic reaction to the epic noun-epithet formulas that formed a distinctive part of his poetic heritage. Before leaving this topic, it should be pointed out that Alcaeus is as free and independent in his handling of these formulas as he was in his treatment of subject matter borrowed from the epic tradition. A few selected examples will serve to illustrate this point.[9] Alcaeus sometimes leaves the vocabulary of the epic formula intact as in the case of "holy Ilium" ("The Fall of Troy" = B 10, line 4; *Iliad* IV, line 46), "aegis-bearing Zeus" (Z 19; *Iliad* I, line 202), and "swift-footed steeds" ("Castor and Polydeuces" = B 2 [a], line 6; *Iliad* II, line 383). Elsewhere, he may retain the Homeric epithet but assign it to a noun of different meaning: Homer's "spirit-devouring strife" (*Iliad* VII, lines 210 and 301) becomes "spirit-devouring sedition" in "Pittacus" (D 12, line 10); Homer's "in trailing robes," an epithet applied exclusively to the Trojan women (*Iliad* VI, line 442; XXII, line 105; VII, line 297), is used by Alcaeus to modify "maidens of Lesbos" in "The Prayer" (G 1, lines 32-33); and with the addition of an intensive prefix and a change of noun Homer's "chilling fear" (*Iliad* IX, line 2) and "chilling flight" (*Iliad* V, line 740) are transformed into "death so chilling" in "Castor and Polydeuces" (B 2 [a]; lines 7-8).[10] Again, Alcaeus may leave undisturbed the fundamental meaning of the Homeric formula, but with the substitution of a different noun of precisely the same denotation: Homer's word for "earth," *gaia* (*Iliad* II, line 699), becomes *chthōn* ("Sisyphus" = B 6 A, line 10) in the phrase "dark earth"; Homer's "blessed gods" (*Iliad* I, lines 339, 406, 599) appears as "blessed immortals" in "The Prayer" (G 1, line 4); and Alcaeus's "bay steeds" ("The Fall of Troy" = B 10, line 14) employs *pōloi* rather than Homer's *hippoi* (*Iliad* XI, line 680) as the word for "steeds."

Too, Alcaeus extends his use of phrases endowed with an epic tone beyond the confines of simple noun-epithet combinations, and here also in this broader usage the introduction of epic phraseology is not limited to epic or mythological contexts.[11] "The Fall of Troy" (B 10) narrates the consummation of the marriage of Peleus and Thetis with the statement "and he loosed the maiden's girdle" (lines 9-10), which is closely modeled on a narrative statement in the *Odyssey* (Book XI, line 245): "and he loosed her maiden girdle." Alcaeus has subjected his model to stylistic and linguistic revision; for example, he has added an augment to its verb and has replaced *zōnē*, the epic word for "girdle," with *zōma*, a word of the same denotation but of differing metrical value. Nevertheless, the revision does not obscure the Homeric origin of Alcaeus's narrative remark. Again, in "Helen" (N 1) "the heart within her breast" (lines 3-4) and the reference to "chariots in the dust" (line 15) call to mind innumerable instances of the same vocabulary in Homer;[12] and "from under the eyebrows" at verse 24 of "Ajax and Cassandra" (Q 1) is a recurrent prepositional phrase throughout the *Iliad* and the *Odyssey*.[13]

The Homeric borrowings of this second type in "The Fall of Troy," "Helen," and "Ajax and Cassandra," all of which employ epic subject matter, are matched by similar borrowings in poems of nonepic context. In "Exile" (G 2), for example, the main verb in verses 32-33 ("Where maidens of Lesbos being judged for beauty/ process in trailing robes....") rings of Homer.[14] And the same is emphatically true of two descriptive phrases in "The Armory" (Z 34). Alcaeus's "shining helmets from which white horsehair plumes nod down" (lines 3-4) must ultimately derive from Homer's "well-fashioned helmet/ with the horse-hair crest, and the plumes nodded terribly above it."[15] (The Homeric description occurs in two of the *Iliad's* most famous arming scenes, that of Paris and that of Patroclus.) In this same poem Alcaeus's description of greaves as "a defense against a powerful missile" (line 5) is reminiscent of Homer's description of the robe with which Aphrodite shielded Aeneas as "a defense against missiles" (*Iliad* V, lines 315-16); also, of Homer's "a defense against spears," a phrase used to describe a piece of defensive armor at *Iliad* IV, line 137.

So far we have been examining the exclusively stylistic affect of Homeric repetitions and reminiscences on Alcaeus's poetic diction. Alcaeus introduced and, where necessary, revised such epic borrowings in a manner that did not entail his tampering with the linguistic content of his Aeolic vernacular. This, however, is far from the whole story, for there is considerable evidence of a subtle yet comprehensive influence of epic vocabulary, morphology, and metrical practices on Alcaeus's native dialect. The influence I am speaking of is stylistic but goes far deeper than mere style. It involves the use of words, forms, and scansions that are foreign to Aeolic Greek and are imported from the epic dialect. Again, the influence cuts across contextual lines and subtly pervades Alcaeus's diction and style.[16]

First, Alcaeus has incorporated into his poetic vocabulary a relatively small number of epic words that were foreign to the Aeolic vernacular in which he wrote.[17] In each instance that will be cited, it is certain that Alcaeus had at his disposal a poetically usable Aeolic word of precisely the same meaning and, therefore, used the lexically different word out of choice rather than necessity. (Certainty is readily afforded in most instances by the existence of the vernacular word in the poems of Sappho and elsewhere in the Alcaean corpus.) Interestingly enough, whether by chance or design, three of these words appear in the brief span of the two fragmentary stanzas that have survived from the Hymn to the Hebrus (B 13): *gaia* ("earth," *gā* in the vernacular but *gaia* again in Z 32), *parthenika* ("maiden," *parthenos* in the vernacular but *parthenika* again in "Ajax and Cassandra" [Q 1], line 20), and *hydōr* ("water," *hydōr* with short first syllable in the vernacular, the epic *hydōr* being metrically expedient in the Hymn to the Hebrus). At B 1 (d), line 7 and B 7 (a), line 6, there are examples of an epic word for "citizen," *poliatas*, whose Aeolic equivalent is *politas*; and the epic *teos*

("your") appears once (item 310 in Lobel and Page's edition)
instead of Aeolic *sos*. Also, at B 16, line 15 the epic word for
"house," *dōma*, has replaced the vernacular *domos*. Finally, epic
words for "and" (*ēde*, line 2) and "easily" (*rēa*, line 7) occur in
"Castor and Polydeuces" (B 2 [a]). The latter exhibits an interesting concession to the vernacular in that Alcaeus has Aeolicized
the epic spelling *rheia* into *rēa*, just as he did in the case of
parthenika (epic *parthenikē*) and *poliatas* (epic *poliētēs*).

Alcaeus's incorporation of non-Aeolic, epic vocabulary into
his poetic diction, while it served in subtle fashion to enhance the
Homeric tone of his style, nevertheless had only a superficial
effect on the linguistic content of his Aeolic vernacular; for he
Aeolicized the spelling and, therefore, the enunciation of this
epic vocabulary whenever they clashed with the practices of his
vernacular. The linguistic effect is, however, far more radical
and profound when he introduces into his diction epic flectional
forms that are alien to the Aeolic dialect; and it was perhaps a
fear of doing linguistic violence to his vernacular that caused
Alcaeus to exercise great restraint when tampering with the
inflections native to his dialect. The evidence indicates that it
was a practice rarely used, though there is no reason to believe
that it was confined to a particular type of poem or to a particular
context. We must suppose that Alcaeus was motivated by
aesthetic considerations more subtle than those of form or
subject matter.[18]

Though Z 44 consists of only two imperfectly preserved verses,
it grants a telescopic view of the restraint with which epic
flectional forms are employed by Alcaeus. This fragment contains
five nouns and adjectives in the genitive singular, of which only
erchomenoio ("coming"), a participle modifying "spring" in
the phrase "of flowery spring coming" (*ēros anthemoentos
erchomenoio*), exhibits an epic inflection. In fact, this genitive in
-*oio* is the single example of epic morphology in Z 44, which
offers a distinctively Aeolic form of the article in the genitive
singular (*tō*) and the Aeolic rather than the epic word for
"spring" (*ēr* rather than *ear*). Had Alcaeus wished to be less
restrained in his use of epic elements, he could certainly have
revised the word order of Z 44 so as to accommodate the epic
word for "spring," whose genitive singular he actually uses elsewhere in the phrase "gates of spring" (*earos pylai;* P 2 [b],
line 3). An example of similar restraint is afforded by "Helen"

(N 1), where in verse 12 Alcaeus chooses an epic flectional form of "many" (*poleas*, accusative plural) but reverts to an Aeolic form in verse 16 (*polloi*, nominative plural)—and this despite his Homeric subject matter and the availability of the distinctively epic nominative plural *polees* as a substitute for *polloi*. Alcaeus must have felt that *poleas* alone, without the addition of *polees*, made a sufficient contribution to the particular degree of epic tone he was striving for in "Helen."

B 16 is so mutilated as to rule out any attempt to accurately reconstruct its content. Its surviving words and phrases, however, give abundant indication of a clear and comprehensive epic tone. In addition to the Homeric epithets "holy" ("holy Babylon," line 10) and "chilling" (line 12), there occurs in the phrase "house of Hades" (line 15) the Homeric word for house (*dōma* instead of the Aeolic *domos*) and an epic inflection for the genitive "Hades" (*Aidao* instead of Aeolic *Aida*). Elsewhere, Alcaeus prefers the vernacular form of the genitive singular of nouns of this type: *Latoïda*, "son of Leto" (D 9, line 3) and *Kronida*, "son of Cronus" (Z 64). In passing, we may note an epic inflection of the word for "city-state" in a poem too fragmentary to permit even speculation as to content (B 9, line 18): *polēos* in place of Aeolic *polios*.

One hallmark of Homeric morphology is the frequent omission of verb augment, both syllabic and temporal. Alcaeus, again with his customary linguistic restraint, applies this epic practice;[19] and for our immediate purposes it may be explained as follows. Verbs in Aeolic as well as the other Greek dialects normally exhibit augment in the imperfect and aorist tenses, both past tenses. If the present tense of the verb begins with a consonant, then the augment takes the form of an epsilon (*e* in English transliteration) prefixed to the verb in its imperfect and aorist tenses. For example, at verse nine of "Helen" (N 1) Alcaeus uses the verb *peithō* ("I persuade") in the imperfect. The normal, vernacular form of this imperfect would be *epeithe* ("was persuading"; the subject of the verb is uncertain): Alcaeus, however, has omitted the augment and written *peithe*. The meaning remains unchanged, but by employing a form foreign to Aeolic and to be expected in Homer Alcaeus has introduced a strikingly epic element. With regard to temporal augment, it occurs in the imperfect and aorist tenses of verbs beginning with a vowel rather than a consonant, and takes the form of a lengthening of that vowel. Alcaeus offers a single example of the omission of this augment, in Z 12, in a phrase reminiscent of a Homeric phrase which also omits the temporal augment from the same verb used by Alcaeus. Alcaeus employs an unaugmented *eleto* (instead of the augmented *eileto*) in the remark that somebody "stole away" somebody else's "wits," just as Homer does at *Iliad* VI, line 234: "but Zeus the son of Kronos stole away the wits of Glaukos."[20]

We must bear in mind, however, that Alcaeus does not confine his epicisms to epic or mythological subject matter. In fact, he does not hesitate to introduce an unaugmented aorist and, therefore, an epic tone into his announcement that a political enemy is dead (Z 8): "Now's the time to get drunk and with some vigor/ to drink, for Myrsilus has died, indeed he has...." The Greek verb translated as "has died" is *katthane*, a syllabically unaugmented form of *katethane* (*kat* being a prefix and *thane* the verb proper; the augment is attached directly to the latter) that is distinctively epic in tone. The context, however, is either Homeric ("The Fall of Troy" [B 10], line 13) or mythological (Hymn to Hermes [item 308 in Lobel and Page's edition] and Hymn to Eros [Z 3]) when Alcaeus uses the unaugmented *gennato* ("bore," "gave birth to"; the normal Aeolic form is *egennato*) in reference, respectively, to the births of Achilles, Hermes, and Eros.

There remains for consideration Alcaeus's limited use of metrical practices common in Homer and not normally admitted in Aeolic verse. The type of thing he does may be illustrated from his use of epic correption and synizesis, both regular features of epic prosody.[21] Correption is the artificial shortening of a long syllable that is final, open, and followed by a word beginning with a vowel. For correption to be admissible, *all* three criteria must be satisfied; but even then the epic poet, should his versification so require, may reject correption and keep the syllable long. There is only one sure example of correption in the remains of Alcaeus's poetry, though we may reasonably surmise, in view of his over-all incorporation of epic features into his style and diction, that he used it somewhat more widely than the accidents of preservation reveal, but always with great restraint. The scansion of the single verse composing Z 43 ("Wine, dear boy, and truth") offers a recognizable and not unexpected Aeolic metrical scheme, if we accept the cor-

$$\bar{} \quad \smile \; \bar{} \; \smile \; \bar{} \quad \smile\smile \quad \bar{} \quad \smile \; \smile \; \bar{}\smile\bar{}$$

reption of *kai* into *kai*: *oinos, ō phile pai, kai alāthea*. On the other hand, if we deny corruption and insist on the normal Aeolic scansion of *kai* as long, the verse becomes metrically incomprehensible.

Synizesis occurs when two adjacent, open syllables that are normally pronounced and scanned separately must be combined so as, in a particular instance, to be pronounced and scanned as a single syllable. Alcaeus offers a sure example of synizesis in a mythological context, in verse eleven of "Castor

and Polydeuces" (B 2 [a]): $\bar{} \; \smile \; \bar{} \quad \bar{} \; \smile \; \bar{}$ *argaleai d'en nykti*... ("And in troublous night...."). These words begin the third verse of a Sapphic Stanza, and this verse must begin metrically with a cretic ($- \smile -$). It is, therefore, certain that Alcaeus, by means of synizesis, altered the pronunciation and scansion of the

first word in verse 11 from its normal form ($\bar{} \; \smile\smile \; \bar{}$ *argaleai*, "trouble-

some") to $\bar{} \; \smile \; \bar{}$ *argaleai* (the final two syllables *e* and *ai* being combined into a single syllable), in order to produce the cretic demanded by the inexorable rules of Aeolic versification. Alcaeus, however, does not confine his use of Homeric metrical license to epic subject matter. The instance of correption previously cited was in a nonepic context, and there is an occurrence of synizesis in a poem whose subject is equally nonepic. Verse 5 of "The Armory" (Z 34) ends with a description of greaves

as "a defense against a powerful missile" ($\bar{} \; \smile \; \bar{} \quad \smile \; \bar{} \quad \smile \; \bar{}$ *arkos ischyrō beleos*). The metrical scheme of this poem requires an iambic metron ($\smile - \smile -$) at the end of each line: this metron is achieved

if synizesis is applied to $\smile \; \smile\smile$ *beleos* (the word for "missile"), so

that it becomes $\smile \; \bar{}$ *beleos*.[22]

Alcaeus never allowed himself to be used by the epic tradition when he turned to it for subject matter; he took what he wanted and freely adapted it to his lyric needs and the native verse forms in which he chose to compose. The same is true of his use of Homeric diction. He borrowed some Homeric formulas and used others as models for the creation of phrases of epic tone; he incorporated, though always with restraint and discretion, epic vocabulary, morphology, and metrical licenses into his

diction and versification. The total stylistic result is a carefully
designed literary dialect of his own creation. The base and the
overwhelmingly dominant linguistic content of this dialect is, of
course, his Aeolic vernacular. He has, however, endowed this
vernacular with an epic tone at all levels. The tone is clearest
on the surface of his poetic diction, when he inserts noun-epithet
phrases of Homeric type. It becomes somewhat softer with his
use of other, more general phrases that are reminiscent of epic
formulas. And though the epic tone is even fainter when introduced into his vocabulary and morphology, its effect in these
areas is paradoxically more profound; for it here touches the
linguistic base of his dialect. The tone, however, is reduced to
no more than a subtle hint in the area of metrics and versification.
It may well be that Alcaeus's most original artistic achievement
was the creation of an intensely personal literary dialect that
may be described as a slightly epicized Aeolic and that was
designed exclusively for his own poetic needs.

II   *The Derivation of a Theme*

We have already observed on Alcaeus's part an interest in
things Boeotian; for two of his Hymns, those to Athena Itonia
and to Eros, celebrated local cult deities of Boeotia.[23] In addition, Alcaeus owes a clear and demonstrable literary debt to
Hesiod, who lived in Ascra, a town at the foot of Mount Helicon
in Boeotia, whither the poet's father had migrated from Cyme
in the Aeolid of Asia Minor. Hesiod's dates are far from certain, and we can do no better than place his lifetime during the
late ninth or eighth century B.C.[24] The only chronological matter of immediate importance, however, is that he decisively ante-
dated Alcaeus. Hesiod's *Works and Days* and *Theogony* are
both composed in the epic dialect and both employ the meter
of epic poetry, the dactylic hexameter.[25] It is verses 582-88 of
the former poem that will now be our primary concern, for they
are the direct source and inspiration for the extant portion of
Alcaeus's "Summer" (Z 23).

These seven verses of the *Works and Days* form the opening
half of a passage in which Hesiod describes, first (lines 582-88),
the salient features of summer and, then (lines 588-96), how he
himself would like to spend his time during the summer. The
surviving part of Alcaeus's "Summer" (Z 23) is an adaptation

of the first half of the Hesiod passage, the description of the features of summer. Since, however, not all of Alcaeus's poem has survived, we may speculate that in its lost portion Alcaeus went on to adapt the rest of the Hesiodic material that was obviously before him. And even if Alcaeus limited his close adaptation to lines 582-88, it is still likely that the second half of Hesiod's description exercised some influence on the lost part of "Summer" (Z 23). For one thing, the opening thematic idea of Alcaeus's poem is derived, as will be shown, from the last rather than from the first half of the Hesiod passage.

So that the reader may see the full extent of the poetic source material Alcaeus was working from when he composed "Summer," I will give the entire *Works and Days* passage, using Hugh G. Evelyn-White's prose translation (a paragraph division will indicate the end of the section that inspired the remains of Alcaeus's poem).

But when the artichoke flowers, and the chirping cicada sits in a tree and pours down his shrill song continually from under his wings in the season of wearisome heat, then goats are plumpest and wine sweetest; women are most wanton, but men are feeblest, because Sirius parches head and knees and the skin is dry through heat.

But at that time let me have a shady rock and wine of Biblis, a clot of curds and milk of drained goats with the flesh of an heifer fed in the woods, that has never calved, and of firstling kids; then also let me drink bright wine, sitting in the shade, when my heart is satisfied with food, and so, turning my head to face the fresh Zephyr, from the everflowing spring . . . thrice pour an offering of water, but make a fourth libation of wine.[26]

The following prose translation of "Summer" (Z 23) may be used to demonstrate the manner in which Alcaeus has reacted to the Hesiod passage. (Pointed brackets around a word indicate that it is a conjecture derived from the *Works and Days*, and a series of three dots that there is either a lacuna or an incomprehensible section in Alcaeus's·text.)[27]

Soak your lungs with wine, for the dogstar's in the sky, and the season is harsh. Everything's athirst through heat, and the cicada chirps sweetly from the leaves and pours down from under his wings his shrill, ⟨continuous⟩ song . . . and the artichoke flowers. Now women are loosest, but men are weak, because Sirius parches head and knees. . . .

Alcaeus's debt to the *Works and Days* is immediately obvious
and beyond need of demonstration. Nevertheless, it deserves to
be examined in more detail. On a purely dramatic level, Alcaeus
has taken the drinking motif from the second half of the Hesiod
passage and emphatically transposed it to the very beginning of
"Summer," though in a decisively abbreviated form. Also, though
Alcaeus appropriates directly much of Hesiod's vocabulary and
phrasing, he does not hesitate to disrupt the order of his source
and place his borrowings in whatever order suits his own needs.
"The artichoke flowers," which opens Hesiod's description, does
not appear until verse 7 of "Summer" (Z 23); and "through
heat" occurs early in Alcaeus's poem, although it is at the very
end of the Hesiod section being adapted. Too, Hesiod's reference
to goats is omitted, and "the dogstar's in the sky" is Alcaeus's
own addition. Finally, there is some revision of the *Works and
Days* vocabulary: for example, Hesiod's "women are most wanton" (*machlotatai*) becomes "women are loosest" (*miarōtatai*),
and Alcaeus changes his source's "men are feeblest" (*aphauro-
tatoi*) into "men are weak" (*leptoi*).

On a metrical and linguistic level, Alcaeus has made whatever
changes were appropriate to the exigencies of his own Aeolic
dialect with its own distinctive meters. Hesiod's dactylic
hexameters have been replaced by major asclepiads, and Alcaeus
has rid his verbal borrowings of all their non-Aeolic morphology.
The following chart will reveal the type of morphological
revision which Alcaeus undertook.

Form in *Works and Days*	Meaning	Form in "Summer" (Z 23)
ligyrēn (line 583)	"shrill"	*ligyran* (line 4)
katacheuetai (line 583)	"pours down"	*kakcheei* (line 4)
aoidēn (line 583)	"song"	*aoidan* (line 4)
hypo (line 588)	"through"	*ypa* (line 2)
kephalēn (line 587)	"head"	*kephalan* (line 8)
gounata (line 587)	"knees"	*gona* (line 8)
azei (line 587)	"parches"	*asdei* (line 9)

A critical enigma is posed by Alcaeus's artistic reaction to his
epic source. We have already seen how he refined his Aeolic
vernacular and transformed it into a personal literary dialect by
the incorporation of epic diction and of epic linguistic and

metrical features. We would, therefore, expect to find a profusion of such epic elements in a poem that is so obvious and so close an adaptation of a set of epic verses. Yet just the opposite is true. Insofar as possible in an adaptation of this sort— one is tempted to say "translation," though this would not be quite accurate—Alcaeus has stripped his borrowings of their epic tone: there is not in "Summer" (Z 23) a single linguistic or metrical feature that is borrowed from the epic. In fact, if the Hesiod passage were not available for comparison, one would never suspect that Alcaeus was composing an adaptation of epic source material rather than an absolutely independent and nonderivative piece of poetry. It is as though Alcaeus was demonstrating his own skill as a poetic craftsman by taking an epic theme and dealing with it in a nonepic manner. The result is a poetic tour de force that is as aesthetically successful as it is technically skillful.[28]

III   *The Debt to Archilochus*

The dictional, linguistic, and metrical refinements of Alcaeus's poetry give proof that his was a technically sophisticated and highly polished art. So also do the skill and adroitness with which he has stylistically disguised the Hesiodic origins of "Summer" (Z 23), a poem whose poetic spontaneity completely belies the derivative nature of its theme. Derivative and conventional themes and motifs permeate the Homeric epic and constitute one of its fundamental features but are somewhat surprising when encountered in the intensely personal atmosphere of Alcaeus's lyrics. Yet having discovered that the theme and motifs of a poem so artistically spontaneous as "Summer" (Z 23) are consciously derivative and owe their spontaneity solely to Alcaeus's poetic genius, the critic is encouraged to search elsewhere among the body of his poetry for similar derivations. There is no other poem that in this respect falls in the category of "Summer," whose origin and poetic inspiration is actually available for comparison. The relation, however, of "Summer" to the *Works and Days* provides a perspective from which to consider Alcaeus's relation to his predecessor Archilochus.

As with Hesiod, Archilochus's dates are the subject of scholarly controversy.[29] (Probably the best that we can do is to assign him to the mid-seventh century B.C.) Also as with Hesiod, this

controversy need not affect the present inquiry; for it is certain
that Archilochus lived before Alcaeus and that his poems were
available for Alcaeus to borrow from. Forced by poverty to leave
his native Paros, Archilochus migrated to the island of Thasos
and earned a living as a mercenary. He met death in battle,
fighting against the Naxians. His life is perhaps summed up in
the elegiac couplet in which he describes himself as both a
warrior and a poet (1): "I am two things: a fighter who
follows the Master of Battles,/ and one who understands the
gift of the Muses' love."[30]

Our immediate concern is with a poem in which Archilochus
blatantly defies the ideals of aristocratic chivalry (6):

> Some barbarian is waving my shield, since I was obliged to
>   leave that perfectly good piece of equipment behind
> under a bush. But I got away, so what does it matter?
>   Let the shield go; I can buy another one equally good.

Both Herodotus (V, 94-95) and Strabo (XIII, 600) inform us
that Alcaeus wrote a poem of similar theme, and in the latter's account there is preserved a short, but unfortunately
corrupt, quotation from the poem in question.[31] According to
these two accounts, during a battle against the Athenians,
Alcaeus threw aside his arms and escaped by fleeing. The
Athenians recovered these arms and hung them in the temple of
Athena at Sigeum. Alcaeus then recorded the whole experience
in a poem addressed to his comrade Melanippus and sent the
poem back to Mytilene to be recited there. The brief quotation
preserved by Strabo is corrupt but one phrase is clear and certain: "Alcaeus is safe."

The tone of Alcaeus's poem was, therefore, similar to that of
Archilochus's: "I threw away my arms and ran away. But who
cares? I survived, and that's all that matters." It is my belief that
both the theme and the tone of Alcaeus's poems were derived
from Archilochus's and that there was more of art than of
sincerity in the Mytilenean's verses. This is not, however, to
deny them poetic spontaneity, and I would imagine that, just
as in "Summer" (Z 23), Alcaeus handled his derived theme
in a fresh and original manner. Indeed, to the aristocratic ideals
defied by Archilochus, Alcaeus seems to have boldly—and we may
suspect rashly—added those of the city-state: on a literal level
he has rejected both chivalry and patriotism. It is, nevertheless,

judicious to regard Alcaeus's poem as fundamentally a literary endeavor based on a derived theme. Since the poem as a whole is lost, it is impossible to say whether he took anything from his model in the way of style or vocabulary. It is, however, safe to assume that Alcaeus rejected Archilochus's elegiacs for an Aeolic verse scheme, since it is his almost unvarying practice to compose only in his native meters.

There are other thematic areas, all of them previously remarked in another context, in which Alcaeus may well have been influenced by his Parian forerunner. Both show a predilection for bestial motifs;[32] and Alcaeus's "fox of crafty mind," to which a man behaving with shrewdness and deceit is compared in "The Fox" (D 11, lines 6-8), immediately calls to mind the "clever fox with shrewd mind" who appears in one of Archilochus's allegorical fables (81). It is a reasonable guess that Alcaeus's Fox was Pittacus,[33] but in neither instance do we really know who is represented by the fox. What is important for present interests is the striking similarity in vocabulary. Noteworthy also is the use by both poets of the Stone of Tantalus to represent a chronic and terrible danger. Archilochus wrote in Fragment 55, "Let not the stone of Tantalus/ overhang this island any longer"; and the scholiast source of Z 42 reveals that Alcaeus was referring to the same stone when he warned "There lies above your head, O son of Aesimus, a great stone."

Finally, we must bear in mind that Alcaeus's impressive nautical allegories were preceded by an Archilochean allegory in which heavy seas symbolize war (56): "Glaukos, look! The open sea is churning to a wash of waves/ deep within. A cloud stands upright over the Gyrean cape,/ signal of a storm, and terror rises from the unforeseen." The explanation of both the fact and the symbolism of this allegory comes from the perceptive Heraclitus, whose *Allegories* was vitally instrumental in our analysis of Alcaeus's nautical allegories.[34] Heraclitus quotes the three verses just translated, and must have had before him Archilochus's entire poem. The modern critic, therefore, can do no better than accept Heraclitus's allegorical explanation of these verses. What is remarkable is that Archilochus's lines by themselves are so poetically spontaneous and vivid as to conceal—one might even say to disguise—their allegorical nature; and were it not for Heraclitus, who was able to analyze them in relation to

the full poem in which they occurred, we would have no grounds
for suspecting the presence of allegory.

Just as Archilochus vividly depicted the advent of his allegorical storm as though it were a real storm, so does Alcaeus
throughout his nautical allegories use imagery vividly appropriate
to a real ship foundering in a real storm. "The Ship:II" (Z 2),
of which somewhat more than two stanzas survive, will be
sufficient to remind the reader of this fact:

> I cannot understand how the winds are set
> against each other. Now from this side and now
> from that the waves roll. We between them
> run with the wind in our black ship driven,
>
> hard pressed and laboring under the giant storm.
> All round the mast-step washes the sea we shipped.
> You can see through the sail already
> where there are opening rents within it.
>
> The forestays slacken. . . .[35]

I would suggest that the realism, vividness, and spontaneity of
this allegorical description were in part derived from an allegorical style contrived and established by Archilochus. And this is
no more than we should expect, for the warrior-poet of Paros
is one of the most original and creative figures in Greek
literature.[36]

IV The Lesbian Antecedents

Alcaeus and Sappho account for Lesbos's literary flourishing.
This, however, is not the full account of the island's poetic
muse, and there is varied evidence, limited in scope but cogent
in total import, that the compositions of these two lyricists are
only the culmination of a long and vibrant tradition of verse
and song. Despite the loss of so much that Alcaeus and Sappho
produced, enough of their work has survived to attest abundantly
to the maturity and sophistication of their metrical and linguistic
techniques; and such testimony, were all other evidence lacking,
would be ample proof of generations of antecedent poetic
activity. Just as with the *Iliad* and the *Odyssey*, artistic refinement places Alcaeus and Sappho at the climax of an antique

tradition. And it is a tradition that must be peculiar to the island of Lesbos, or at least to Aeolis, as is adequately demonstrated by the peculiarly Aeolic nature of the language and the meters in which Alcaeus and Sappho composed. Moreover, as early as Archilochus the island was known for a particular style of flute music and was associated with the Paean, a hymn in honor of Apollo;[37] and an ancient treatise on music reveals that well before the era of Sappho and Alcaeus, Aeolian, and especially Lesbian, singers (*kitharōdoi*) were famous for both the style of their song and the type of lyre they used.[38]

Two of these *kitharōdoi* distinguished themselves as among the great creative figures in the early history of Greek music and lyric poetry. Terpander of Antissa on Lesbos in the generation before Sappho and Alcaeus migrated to Sparta, then a cultural and artistic center, where he won fame not only through his accomplishments and innovations as singer, musician, and poet but also for quelling civil discord.[39] And Arion of Methymna, also on Lesbos, was at the height of his musical and poetic career at about the time Alcaeus and Sappho were born. Arion, just as Terpander, found his fame abroad, far from the shores of Lesbos at the court of Periander in Corinth and in Italy and Sicily. Herodotus credits him with having invented, named, and taught the dithyramb (a choral song to Dionysus) while he was at Corinth.[40]

A tradition of popular song on Lesbos is attested by two separately preserved sets of verses. One, a Sapphic fragment of two lines, is regarded by Bowra as modeled on "a *chanson de toile,* such as girls sang over the loom, lamenting their loves":[41] "Sweet mother, I cannot weave my web; for because of slender Aphrodite I am overcome with desire for a boy." The other is a folk piece which was sung by women at Eresos on the western shores of Lesbos, far from Mytilene: "Grind, hand-mill, grind,/ for even Pittacus used to grind/ when he was king of great Mytilene."[42] This song, though the exact nature of its symbolism and political connotations is unclear, is obviously critical of Pittacus, and, therefore, has affinities with the political invective that characterizes so much of Alcaeus's verse.[43] Despite uncertainty as to the date of the Eresos song, the implication is that the political element in Alcaeus's poetry was to a degree spawned by popular songs that in fact constituted a portion of his literary heritage.

V *Sappho and Alcaeus*

Sappho and Alcaeus share much in common. They were contemporary, from Mytilene, and products of the same aristocratic society.[44] Both composed their poems in, fundamentally, the same dialect and the same meters,[45] and both owe the fragmentary preservation of their poetry to a similar combination of mutilated papyrus texts and quotations by later authors.[46] Also, both freely borrow and imitate epic phraseology, particularly the Homeric noun-epithet formulas.[47] Furthermore, neither has hesitated to modify the morphology, vocabulary, and prosody of his native dialect and meters by a restrained and limited admixture of features which were borrowed from the epic dialect and which were linguistically foreign to their vernacular.

In respect to this very last point, however, a subtle divergence of Sappho from Alcaeus in the area of style and artistic craftsmanship is noticeable.[48] Whereas Alcaeus in general allowed this linguistic admixture to appear in exceedingly small and carefully measured quantities throughout the entire body of his poetry, Sappho excluded it from the vast majority of her poems and confined it to a select body of verse presently represented by fragments from only eight separate poems.[49] (I stress that I am not here referring to phraseology of Homeric tone which does not linguistically alter Sappho's and Alcaeus's Aeolic vernacular, but instead to the use of words, forms, and metrical expedients borrowed from the epic and foreign to the Aeolic dialect and to Aeolic versification, items such as epic correption, genitives with the epic inflection *-oio*, and *parthenika* as the word for "maiden" in place of Aeolic *parthenos*.) Sappho's stylistic reaction to the epic dialect has led Lobel to enunciate the linguistic classification of her poems as either "normal" or "abnormal," normal designating the large bulk of her poetry, which excludes features of the epic dialect, and abnormal that small remainder of poems which admit these epic features. No such distinction may be made for Alcaeus, who, insofar as we can judge from his extant poetry, has consistently preferred a more regular and uniform style.

There is, in addition, enticing, although problematic, evidence that Sappho and Alcaeus enjoyed a certain literary rapport, whose nature unfortunately is as difficult to specify as its extent is to define. The evidence is in the form of two fragments, one among the Sapphic, the other among the Alcaean corpus. The latter (Z 61), though only a single verse, may be appropriately titled "Sappho": "violet-tressed, holy, gentle-smiling Sappho."[50] This is all that has survived from the poem, and we cannot assign the verse to Alcaeus with absolute certainty; for Hephaestion, who quotes it, cites it as an example of an "Alcaic twelve-syllable" and fails to give an express indication as to its author. It has been suggested that Hephaestion's adjective "Alcaic" reflects the verse's authorship rather than helps designate its metrical type, and Lobel and Page along with numerous other editors have assigned it to Alcaeus.[51] We can do no better than accept this editorial judgment, together with that of Bowra, who enthusiastically endorses the invocation's Alcaean authorship.[52] The adjectives applied to Sappho in this verse are certainly not foreign to Alcaeus's style and vocabulary. The Graces are designated as "holy" in Z 63 (*agnai Charites*); and forms of the adjective "holy" (*agnos*) occur in B 9 (line 7) and "Exile" (G 2, line 16), though in these two last-mentioned occurrences the accidents of preservation have not left an appropriate noun for the adjective to modify. Also, the compound epithets "violet-tressed" (*ioploke*) and "gentle-smiling" (*mellichomeide*) call to mind other Alcaean compound epithets, such as those in the phrases "swift-footed steeds" ("Castor and Polydeuces" = B 2, line 6) and "golden-haired Zephyr" (Hymn to Eros = Z 3). The question of authorship aside, the invocation pays rare tribute to Sappho, for she here receives epithets appropriate to diety. *Agnos* ("holy"), as was just remarked, is applied by Alcaeus to the Graces in Z 63; and in general this adjective was reserved for divinities and divine objects prior to the fifth century B.C.[53] Alcaeus's "violet-tressed" (*ioploke*) is reminiscent of the "violet-crowned" (*iostephanos*) assigned Aphrodite in the Homeric Hymn in her honor (number 6, line 17); and "gentle-smiling" (*mellichomeide*) appears to be no more than Alcaeus's own version of *philommeidēs* ("ever-smiling"), which is used exclusively of Aphrodite throughout the *Iliad* and the *Odyssey*. In addition, the accumulation of epithets in Alcaeus's invocation may, for the careful listener, call to mind the similar accumulation of epithets which Aphrodite receives at the opening of Sappho's famous address to her (1): "Richly-enthroned immortal Aphrodite, daughter of Zeus, weaver of wiles...."[54] Sappho is thus invoked by Alcaeus in terms subtly appropriate to Aphrodite. Given the loss of the

rest of the poem which Alcaeus's invocation must have opened,
the implications of this poetic apotheosis cannot but remain
a mystery. Does it represent on Alcaeus's part a religious or
an aesthetic attitude?

The other piece of evidence for a literary rapport between
Sappho and Alcaeus is as much a conundrum as the first. It is
Fragment 137 in Lobel and Page's edition of the Sapphic corpus,
and may be entitled "The Dialogue." Willis Barnstone's translation of the entire fragment will give us a base for comment and
discussion:

> First Speaker:
> I want to speak to you but shame disarms me.
> Second Speaker:
> If you cared for what is upright and good,
> and your tongue were not concocting trouble,
> shame would not be hiding in your eyes
> and you would speak out your real desires.[55]

The primary source for "The Dialogue" is Aristotle (*Rhetoric*,
1367. a), who introduces the above quotation with the following comment: "People are ashamed of what is shameful, whether
they are saying it, doing it, or intending to do it. Compare the
verses Sappho composed, after Alcaeus had said, 'I want to
speak, . . .' "[56]

The simplest and most direct interpretation of Aristotle's
comment is that the first verse in the quotation occurred in a
poem by Alcaeus and that the rest of the quotation is from a
reply to Alcaeus by Sappho. The wording of the comment,
however, leaves open the possibility that the entire fragment
was from a dialogue composed by Sappho, in which she depicted
in verse a conversation between Alcaeus and herself. And some
support is given to this latter possibility by an anonymous
scholion to the effect that Sappho composed a poem in which
she had Alcaeus say, "I want to speak. . . . " Neither explanation
of the relation of the first to the second part of the dialogue
is corroborated by the fact that both parts are in Alcaics. If
the first part was written by Alcaeus himself, we might expect
Sappho to compose her reply in the same metrical scheme, if
for no other reason than to demonstrate her technical mastery
of her art. If, on the other hand, Sappho was the author of the
entire dialogue between Alcaeus and herself, the very fact that

Alcaeus was an interlocutor would render it similarly appropriate for her to choose as the metrical form for the conversation the Alcaic stanza, commonly used by Alcaeus but not elsewhere by Sappho. What is interpretively significant is the simple fact of the Alcaic stanza as the verse form of "The Dialogue." This poem furnishes the only sure example of Alcaics among the entire body of Sappho's poetry,[57] and the modern critic cannot but conclude that their mere presence helps guarantee the general claim of Aristotle and the scholiast that Alcaeus participated in the dialogue, whether literally as the author of its first part or dramatically as an interlocutor to whom Sappho assigned suitable remarks. We may, therefore, confidently follow Maas and Page, who discard as nonsense the queries of the generally unreliable Stephanus.[58] (Stephanus seems to exclude the possibility of Sappho's being the female speaker and questions whether the male speaker is Alcaeus or "someone else.")

In summary, "The Dialogue" confronts the critic with a conversation in poetic form between Alcaeus and Sappho, whether it involves two separate poems assembled by Aristotle or a literary dialogue composed in its entirety by Sappho. As to its content and context, no more is certain than that Alcaeus wants to tell Sappho something of which he is ashamed and that she reprimands him for his shameful intent. What is uncertain is whether the repartee is serious or jovial. Whatever the answer to this and the other questions posed by "The Dialogue," it may be that it was the source of inspiration, either direct or secondary, for a scene on a red-figure vase of the early fifth century B.C. The scene depicts an encounter between Sappho and Alcaeus, each with lyre in hand.[59]

CHAPTER 8

The Verdict of Antiquity

AT some time during the Middle Ages the collected poetry of Alcaeus was irreparably lost.[1] All that remained for later ages were those excerpts quoted by various ancient writers in works that managed to survive to the Renaissance and thereby to be available for modern editions. It was not until the very late nineteenth and the twentieth centuries that these quotations were supplemented by the mutilated, often incomprehensibly mutilated, papyrus texts from Egypt that have so augmented in their own peculiar way more recent editions of the Alcaean corpus. And despite the masterful achievements of such editors as Diehl, Lobel, and Page in uniting in single editions every surviving shred of Alcaeus's poetry, the modern world is still without even one complete poem by him. All this has meant that by mere force of circumstances there never has been (and undoubtedly never will be) a tradition of Alcaean literary influence on post-classical times such as that enjoyed by, say, Alcaeus's lyric heir Horace, whose works have persistently been available in substantial quantity and in the form of entire poems. (Indeed, the bulk of Alcaeus's influence on post-classical times has been exerted indirectly through Horace's *Odes*, which, as will be shown in the last section of this chapter, are permeated with a profound Alcaean influence.)[2] Far different, however, were Alcaeus's literary circumstances in antiquity, when his poetry was intact and circulated in full editions; and it is possible to trace the steady, variegated fabric of his influence throughout Greco-Roman literature and literary criticism, until well into the fourth century A.D. Such tracing will be our immediate interest.

I Critics and Admirers

The name of Alcaeus figures prominently throughout the annals of Greco-Roman literary criticism and evaluation.[3] Near the end of the fourth century B.C. Aristotle's learned and versa-

112

tile pupil Dicaearchus wrote an exegetical commentary on Alcaeus's poetry, and the great Alexandrian scholars Aristophanes of Byzantium and Aristarchus produced editions of his poems. Indeed, at some time during the third or second century B.C. Alexandrian scholarship paid Alcaeus the ultimate tribute of inclusion in the canon of Greek lyric poets (along with Pindar, Bacchylides, Sappho, Anacreon, Stesichorus, Simonides, Ibycus, and Alcman);[4] and the large number of papyri containing poems by Alcaeus or commentaries on his poetry attests to his popularity, at least among critics and educated people, during the early centuries of our era. We are, however, not limited to such general and indirect data for an assessment of Alcaeus's literary reputation among the ancients, for several explicit evaluations of his poetry by Greek and Roman critics have survived.

Let us first examine the evaluation by Dionysius of Halicarnassus, a Greek rhetorician, antiquarian, and literary critic who wrote and taught at Rome during the last third of the first century B.C. In his essay *On Imitation,* Dionysius offers thumbnail critical sketches of a selection of epic, lyric, and dramatic poets.[5] Immediately after treating Pindar, Simonides, and Stesichorus, he turns to Alcaeus, whose poetry is first praised for the elevation, brevity, and forceful charm of its style, then for its figures and absolute clarity, and, finally, for the ethos of its political poems: many of them, when stripped of their meter, are actually political speeches. Though Dionysius's rhetorical bias is apparent (he is interested only in what prospective orators may learn from Alcaeus), it is equally apparent that he admires Alcaeus as a poet and regards him as a classic. It is undoubtedly this very critical judgment that motivates Dionysius in his essay *On Literary Composition* (Chapter 24) to list Alcaeus as a classic representative of the middle style, along with Homer, Stesichorus, Sophocles, Herodotus, Democritus, Plato, Aristotle, and Demosthenes—illustrious company, indeed.[6] Dionysius's judgment, together with its rhetorical bias, is echoed in part by the Roman critic Quintilian, who produced near the end of the first century A.D. a monumental work *On the Education of the Orator.*[7] He too praises Alcaeus on stylistic grounds (X, 1, 63), mentioning brevity, elevation, force, and rhetorical tone. Quintilian, however, adds a moral judgment: he praises Alcaeus's attacks on tyrants as morally edifying but condemns his light and amatory verse as the work of a poet suited for higher things.

No sure products of Alcaeus's erotic muse have survived.[8] But since the secondary tradition that he wrote love poetry is well attested and not limited to Quintilian, it seems appropriate to digress on this tradition; for it calls attention to an Alcaean theme that has not been previously mentioned in this book. Quintilian bluntly censures Alcaeus's amatory verse without giving an indication of either its nature or content. For that, we must turn to Cicero, Horace, and an anonymous scholiast.

Cicero in his *Tusculan Disputations* assigns to one of the speakers an attack on pederasty (and I use this term in its quasi-technical, Greek sense to designate the love of older men for boys). In this attack there is a brief reference to Alcaeus, in which he is praised as an excellent poet and a brave man but condemned for his pederastic verse (IV, 33, 71). The last point is forcefully made in the form of an exclamation: "what things Alcaeus writes about his love for boys!" (*quae de iuvenum amore scribit Alcaeus!*). Quite different in tone is a remark by a speaker in another of Cicero's dialogues. In *De Natura Deorum* Cotta good-naturedly admits to finding the minor physical defects of young men enticing and then cites the delight Alcaeus took in a mole on one of his favorites (I, 28, 79). Cicero, therefore, was familiar with a poem in which Alcaeus must have treated the youth's mole as a foil which set off his beauty, for Cotta remarks: "of course a mole is a physical blemish, but to Alcaeus it appeared as an ornament" (*lumen*).

Cicero's personal attitude toward Alcaeus's erotic poetry need not detain us. What is of immediate importance is that these two Ciceronian passages establish that part—perhaps the bulk—of Alcaeus's love poetry was pederastic rather than heterosexual. This fact is corroborated by the scholiast to D 13, who claims that the "friend" (*philos*) mentioned in this fragment was "Alcaeus's beloved" (the Greek word for "beloved," *erōmenos*, is masculine in gender). And further corroboration is offered by Horace, who says of Alcaeus (*Odes* I, 32, lines 10-12): "and that dark-eyed, / Dark-haired young Lycus he adored." Alcaeus, therefore, wrote an amatory poem, or poems, addressed to a young man named Lycus. The same Horatian Ode, however, raises the possibility that at least some of Alcaeus's love poetry was heterosexual, for in the two verses directly preceding those just quoted Horace writes (lines 9-10): "Still he [Alcaeus] praised.../ ... Venus, at whose side/ Cupid clings close...."[9]

With this background we may now search the Alcaean corpus for evidence of the presence of his erotic muse. If she ever appeared in heterosexual form, as Horace's Ode might lead us to suspect, it was in verses no longer extant;[10] for all vestiges of her presence involve references to men, apparently young men. We have already mentioned the "friend" of D 13, who was invited to dine "on kid and pork." The scholiast may or may not be correct in his exegesis of D 13. In the case of "Menon" (Z 45), there is no scholion to aid our interpretation, although the tone of the poem strikes me as characteristic of Greek pederastic literature: "I bid someone invite the graceful Menon, / if joy of banquet is to come my way." Of similar tone are two one-line fragments, "Dinnomenes" (Z 53): "and you drain a cup sitting beside Dinnomenes" and Z 43: "Wine, dear boy, and truth."[11] Some support is given to classifying Z 43 as pederastic by Theocritus's twenty-ninth Idyll, a love poem addressed to a youth by Theocritus in the guise of an older man. This Idyll is composed in Aeolic Greek and an Aeolic meter and quotes Z 43 in its opening verse.

So much for Alcaeus's erotic muse. It is futile to speculate whether his addresses and references to such persons as Bycchis and Melanippus involve anything more than partisan camaraderie.[12] Let us now return to the theme from which Quintilian led us astray—namely, the evaluation of Alcaeus as a poet by ancient critics. The last name on our list of critics is the Demetrius who passes as the author of an essay *On Style*, which was probably written during the first century B.C. or the first century A.D.[13] Demetrius claims that a graceful style may be achieved by diction or by metaphor (142) and then quotes a short passage from Alcaeus's "Summer" (Z 23) to illustrate his point. Alcaeus's diction and metaphors have already been singled out for special treatment in this book, and it is not surprising to find Demetrius citing Alcaeus to illustrate the effective use of these two ingredients of his poetic style.

Though some ancient critics might question the morality of Alcaeus's erotic verse, they universally admire him as a poet and as a master stylist. Another gauge of his literary reputation during classical antiquity is the use of his poetry for incidental quotations and of his name for passing references by a chronologically diverse group of authors. The special case of Alcaeus's literary influence on Horace, since it will presently receive separate treatment, will be temporarily excluded from comment.

The earliest in this group of authors is the Athenian comic poet Aristophanes, who lived during the latter half of the fifth and the early part of the fourth century B.C. In one of the fragments of the *Banqueters* a character instructs someone to "select a drinking song by Alcaeus or Anacreon and sing it to me,"[14] and in the *Thesmophoriazusae* (lines 159-67), Alcaeus is praised, along with Ibycus, Anacreon, and Phrynichus, as a poet of gentle manners and soft attire. Also, in the *Wasps* (lines 1234-35) Philocleon quotes an Atticized version of two verses of H 2. Again, in the fourth century B.C. we find the philosopher Aristotle simultaneously citing Alcaeus and Sappho to illustrate a point in the *Rhetoric* (1367^a 7-15).[15]

The prose essay and the dialogue, as cultivated during the first century B.C. by Cicero in Latin and over a century later by Plutarch in Greek, drew amply from earlier poetry for references and quotations of the same ornamental variety considered in the preceding paragraph. We have already noted in another connection two Ciceronian examples, those from the *Tusculan Disputations* (IV, 33, 71) and the *De Natura Deorum* (I, 28, 79). In each Cicero added stylistic adornment to a dialogue by assigning to a speaker a reference—in the former, to Alcaeus, Anacreon, and Ibycus; in the latter, to Alcaeus alone.   Numerous other examples are furnished by Plutarch. Three occur in the sophisticated and urbane conversations grouped together under the comprehensive title *Table-Talk*: at 647 E a speaker quotes, somewhat inaccurately and merely to adorn a point of scientific fact, from "The Plea" (B 18); at 726 B a remark by Soclarus indicates that a sobriquet applied by Alcaeus to Pittacus (*zophodorpidas*, "dusk-diner") was a common object of exegetical speculation; and, finally, at 697 F-698 A the first line of "Summer" (Z 23) is thrown into the conversation as a verse familiar to all educated men. Two more such citations appear in Plutarch's *Amatorius*, a lengthy dialogue concerning Eros. At 765 E the digressional remarks about Eros's parentage in Alcaeus's Hymn to Eros (Z 3), remarks accompanied by a three-line quotation from the poem, reveal Alcaeus's verses as a regular subject for critical explication among literary scholars. The second of the *Amatorius* citations, which involves "The People's Choice" (Z 24), conveniently illustrates the manner in which learned and urbane prose writers such as Cicero and Plutarch incorporate into their dialogues and essays references to earlier poets:[16] "The most eminent of poets, legislators, philosophers, join together in enrolling Eros among the gods 'With one voice of great approval,' as Alcaeus says the people of Mytilene elected Pittacus tyrant. So we see Eros chosen as king, chief magistrate, and harmonizer by Hesiod, Plato, Solon" (*Amatorius* 763 E).[17]

In the generation after Plutarch's death, we find Aelius Aristides, the great rhetorician of the second century A.D., summarizing Alcaeus on two, and possibly three, occasions.[18] And near the very end of this century the learned and sophisticated atmosphere of Plutarch's *Table-Talk* was revived in Athenaeus's *Deipnosophistai* ("The Specialists on Dining"), a dialogical tour de force of fifteen books, in which dinner guests of prodigious memory discuss an endless variety of topics and quote with great fluency from antecedent Greek literature. Alcaeus figures prominently among the authors quoted. In addition to being the subject of three references that do not involve quotation, he is represented by thirty-nine-odd verses quoted from fourteen separate poems.[19] And these citations impressively include at XIV, 627a, seven consecutive verses of "The Armory" (Z 34), as well as a two-page disquisition on Alcaeus's references to drinking (X, 430), in which the speaker quotes twenty-three verses from eight different poems.

Alcaeus thus achieved the status of a "classic" early in antiquity and consistently maintained this reputation. He was read, cited, discussed, and evaluated by a variety of ancient authors and critics, Roman as well as Greek; and we have traced the evidence for this fact from the fifth century B.C. down through the second century A.D. That this process continued much longer is attested, in the fourth century A.D., by the orator Himerius's commendatory summary of the Hymn to Apollo,[20] and by the emperor Julian's assessment of Anacreon, Alcaeus, and Archilochus. Julian begins his satire on himself as follows (*Misopogon* 337 A-B): "Anacreon the poet composed many delightful songs; for a luxurious life was alloted to him by the Fates. But Alcaeus and Archilochus of Paros the god did not permit to devote their muse to mirth and pleasure. For constrained as they were to endure toil, now of one sort, now of another, they used their poetry to relieve their toil, and by abusing those who wronged them they lightened the burdens imposed on them by Heaven."[21]

Finally, Julian's teacher, the rhetorician Libanius, adorns one of his orations in the Plutarchan manner with an ornamental quotation from Alcaeus's "The Sword" (Z 27).[22]

II *Historical and Other Uses*

Stylistic ornamentation is one thing. Alcaeus was, in addition, incidentally quoted or appealed to for purposes of illustration by a great variety of literary critics, historical writers, grammarians, metricians, and lexicographers. For example, the Heraclitus who wrote the study of allegory already discussed in two previous chapters illustrates his basic explanation of what "allegory" signifies with citations of Archilochus, Alcaeus, Anacreon, and Homer.[23] Of the twenty-three verses quoted by Heraclitus in this context (*Allegories,* Chapter 5), twelve are from Alcaeus. Also, Hephaestion in his metrical studies (probably written during the second century A.D.) quotes nineteen-odd verses by Alcaeus.[24] Alcaeus's Aeolic Greek (which was, of course, Sappho's as well), distinctive as it was for its meters, vocabulary, and morphology, quite naturally attracted metricians, lexicographers, and grammarians. Historical writers, too, found him a valuable primary source, and the manner in which he was employed by such writers will be our next concern.

The historian Herodotus (fifth century B.C.) offers a short account of the seventh-century conflict between Athens and Mytilene for control of Sigeum in the Troad (Book V, 94-95). Denys Page speculates that "the poems of Alcaeus were presumably the principal ultimate source" of the information furnished by Herodotus.[25] The poetry of Alcaeus is too imperfectly preserved to permit us to test the full accuracy of Page's suggestion. It is certain, however, that Herodotus had consulted at least one poem by Alcaeus, for in 95 he writes: "Amongst the various incidents of this war, one in particular is worth a mention: in the course of a battle in which the Athenians were victorious, the poet Alcaeus ran away; he succeeded in getting clear, but left his weapons in the hands of the victors, who hung them up in the temple of Athena at Sigeum. Alcaeus wrote some verses, describing his little accident to his friend Melanippus, and sent it to him at Mytilene."[26] Herodotus here borrows from Alcaeus for quasi-literary purposes—to give color, as well as additional historical detail, to his narrative of events.

More purely scientific and historical is the use Aristotle, in the fourth century B.C., makes of "The People's Choice" (Z 24). In Book III of the *Politics* (1285ᵃ 29-1285ᵇ 2), Aristotle describes a type of monarchy that he designates as an "elective tyranny" (*hairetē tyrannis*) and then cites Pittacus as a ruler who held this type of tyranny. Then, Aristotle quotes the following passage from "The People's Choice" to justify this claim that Pittacus gained the tyranny through an elective process: "the base-born / Pittacus over that docile and ill-starred city / did they in mobs establish as tyrant, amidst shouts of praise." Pittacus is Aristotle's sole example of a man who was *elected* tyrant, and the fact of his election is derived solely from Alcaeus's poem.

The geographer Strabo, who wrote in Greek during the latter half the first century B.C. and the early years of the first century A.D., was one of Alcaeus's most ardent—and critical—readers. Strabo's attitude toward Alcaeus is in a sense summarized in his discussion of Mytilene at XIII, 2, 2-3. After his geographical description of Mytilene, Strabo lists and briefly characterizes her most famous offspring. At the head of the list stand Pittacus, Alcaeus together with his brother Antimenidas, and Sappho. Elegantly worked into the syntax of the reference to Antimenidas is a combination summary-quotation of a portion of "The Sword" (Z 27). This literary tribute to Alcaeus is appropriately followed by an indication that Alcaeus's stasiotic poems furnish historical information about Mytilene's series of *tyrannoi*. Strabo then, however, raises the suspicion that Alcaeus himself coveted the tyranny—in my opinion, a not unlikely possibility—and rejects Alcaeus's pejorative characterizations of Pittacus, pointing out that Pittacus used the tyranny to crush the disruptive noble factions and then gave Mytilene back her independence (*autonomia*). Strabo thus admired Alcaeus as a poet—otherwise he would not have used a portion of "The Sword" for stylistic ornamentation—but regarded him as a historical source of questionable reliability.

Admiration is the keynote of Strabo's citation at XIII, 1, 51, where he first serves his geographical purposes by observing that "Alcaeus calls Antandrus a city of the Leleges" and then, quite superfluously for these purposes, quotes the Alcaean verse he has just summarized: "Antandrus, first city of the Leleges" (Z 13). Admiration reinforced by antiquarian and historical interest prompts the citations at XIV, 2, 27 and XIII, 1, 38. In the former

passage verses by Anacreon and Alcaeus are adduced to demonstrate that "Carian" is an epithet commonly applied to several
items of military gear. (The Alcaean quotation is Z 65: "and
brandishing a Carian helmet-crest.") In the latter Strabo narrates the incident of Herodotus V, 95: that Alcaeus threw away
his arms and fled during combat against the Athenians at Sigeum,
and then announced in a poem dispatched to Mytilene that
"Alcaeus is safe," though the Athenians have hung up his arms
in the temple of Athena. Strabo must have had Alcaeus's poem
before him, for he offers a summary-quotation of part of it. (The
text of Strabo is so corrupt at this point that it is impossible to
decipher the entire quotation, which was probably two lines in
length.)[27] Elsewhere (IX, 2, 29 and 33), admiration gradually
yields to adverse criticism of Alcaeus's geographical knowledge
of Boeotia. At 29 Strabo admiringly quotes four full verses of
Alcaeus's Hymn to Athena (Z 1), when a mere phrase from
the last of these verses would have sufficed to make the point
that Alcaeus refers to the Boeotian river Cuarius as the "Coralius." But it is not until 33 that it becomes apparent that Strabo
regarded Alcaeus's designation of the river as a misnomer: "But
Alcaeus is wrong, for just as he perverted the name of the River
Cuarius, so he falsified the position of Onchestus, placing it near
the extremities of Helicon, although it is at quite a distance from
the mountain."[28]

The impression created by Strabo's Alcaean citations is that
he had read Alcaeus carefully and extensively. The accuracy of
this impression is corroborated by I, 2, 30, where in a passing
remark Strabo reveals his knowledge of a poem in which Alcaeus
wrote of a trip to Egypt: Alcaeus tells us, Strabo observes, that
he visited Egypt, but he fails to mention that the Nile has several
mouths.

We have traced from the fifth century B.C. down to the early
years of the first century A.D. the use made of Alcaeus's poetry
by several varieties of historical writers, the historian Herodotus,
Aristotle in the guise of political theorist, and the geographer
Strabo. To this group we may add the biographer Diogenes
Laertius, who wrote in the first half of the third century A.D.
a work entitled the *Lives of the Philosophers*. Diogenes twice
draws biographical information from Alcaeus. In his *Life of
Pittacus* (I, 81) he straightforwardly catalogues and comments
on various disparaging epithets which Alcaeus applied to Pittacus.

Each epithet is cited in isolation, without any quoting of its surrounding context, and Diogenes's interests are exclusively biographical. Stylistic ornamentation, however, is as important as biographical interest at I, 31 of the *Life of Thales.* There Diogenes makes a passing reference to Aristodemus of Sparta and appends to it two verses from Alcaeus, in which the Aeolic poet quotes a remark once made by Aristodemus ("A Saying of Aristodemus" = Z 37). Here, as in the case of Herodotus's reference to Alcaeus and of several of the Strabo citations, a later historical writer cites the earlier poet for more than purely historical reasons.

III   *Alcaeus and Horace*

The account of Alcaeus's influence on the Latin poet Horace, who was during the last forty years of the pagan era one of the brilliant luminaries of Augustan literature, has been reserved for special treatment, since no single Alcaean influence equals this one in either extent or profundity.[29] Too, no greater tribute to Alcaeus has survived from all antiquity than the fact that Horace both judged him worthy of imitation and, by his own emphatic testimony, found in him a primary source of poetic inspiration. Before venturing into this account, three points of reference merit preliminary comment. First, we are here concerned not with Horace's entire literary output, only with Horace as a lyric poet in the narrow sense of the word, that is, with the Horace of the *Odes;* for the influence under scrutiny is that of one *lyric* poet on another and is, therefore, confined to the *Odes.* Secondly, though the complexity of metrical considerations excludes them from anything more than cursory attention, it is strikingly indicative of profound technical influence that Aeolic meters overwhelmingly predominate in Horace's *Odes* and that his favorite metrical scheme is the Alcaic Stanza.[30] Finally, the literary data about to be examined are fundamentally different from any that have so far appeared in this chapter. They reach in depth as well as in scope far beyond mere borrowings or statements of praise and approval, and will reveal Alcaeus as one of Horace's literary saints, as a poet's poet without peer. Given two vantage points, Horace's *Odes* and Alcaeus's poetry, we will choose the former as furnishing the appropriate critical perspective and will divide the pertinent Horatian material into

two categories, that exhibiting explicit references to Alcaeus and
that offering indentifiable borrowings without explicit references.

Some three years after the publication of the *Odes* in question
(Books I-III, published in 23 B.C.), Horace near the end of his
first book of *Epistles* speaks with pride of his literary debt to
Alcaeus (I, 19, lines 21-34). This passage opens with "I was the
first to plant/ My feet on an untrodden path; I went forward
freely,/ Not tracing another man's steps. Who trusts in himself/
Will rule the swarm as its king. . . ." And after discussing his
use of Archilochus in the *Epodes*, Horace turns to that of Alcaeus
in his *Odes*: "Alcaeus transformed/ His model [Archilochus], and
I, the lyric poet of Latium,/ Have brought in turn Alcaeus to
people's attention,/ Which no one had done before. . . ."[31]

It is not only in retrospect that Horace recognizes his debt to
and use of Alcaeus as a model and source of inspiration. The
Odes themselves contain striking examples of such explicit
recognition. The thirty-second *Ode* of Book I is a four-stanza
prayer addressed to Horace's lyre, and the lyre of this poem
symbolizes that of Horace's lyric poetry which is inspired by
Alcaeus.[32] Horace first invokes "my lyre,"

> You whom the Lesbian patriot [i.e., Alcaeus]
> First tuned and never once forgot;
> For though he hotly drew his sword
> On battlefields and, storm-driven, moored
> His boat off beaches soaked with brine,
> Still he praised Bacchus and the nine
> Muses and Venus, at whose side
> Cupid clings close, and that dark-eyed,
> Dark-haired young Lycus he adored.

These verses recognize Alcaeus's poetry as a wellspring of
lyric inspiration, and pay tribute to its author by a brief but
comprehensive summary of its basic content. The final stanza
of the Ode gives full expression to both the depth of the inspiration and the intensity of the tribute:

> Lyre, welcome guest at the high board
> Of Jove, Apollo's shining sign
> Of godhead, blessed anodyne
> Of care—whenever I have made
> Due invocation give me aid.

In *Odes* II, 13, Horace again pays explicit tribute to the poet of Mytilene. After describing a narrow escape from death, Horace remarks (lines 21-28) that he almost joined the dead and saw

> ... the blest in their divine
> Seclusion, Sappho on the Aeolian lyre
>
> Mourning the cold girls of her native isle,
> And you, Alcaeus, more full-throatedly
> Singing with your gold quill of ships, exile
> And war, hardship on land, hardship at sea.

At first it appears that Alcaeus must share this tribute equally with Sappho; for Horace adds, "The admiring shades accord the reverent hush/ Due to them both..." (lines 29-30). It quickly becomes clear, however, where Horace's literary preferences lie; for the remainder of the poem (lines 30-40) focuses exclusively on Alcaeus. Horace locks his poetic vision on Alcaeus with "when the theme is war/ And tyrants banished, then the elbowing crush/ Thickens, the ghostly bearers thirst for more" (lines 30-32), then amplifies with "No wonder" (line 33) and a reference to the creatures mesmerized by Alcaeus's lyrics (lines 33-36): "the hundred-headed Hell-dog" and "the snakes that braid the Furies' hair in loops." And Alcaeus's lyre, we are informed in the Ode's final stanza, works its poetic magic not only on shades and monsters: it can also seduce Orion from the chase and "beguile Prometheus and the sire/ Of Pelops of their torments...."

In these explicit references to Alcaeus, Horace is expressing more than justifiable pride in his own achievements and respectful praise of his model. He speaks of Alcaeus with a religious fervor, and one senses an almost mystical rapport with the ancient poet of Mytilene. No such relation existed between Horace and Sappho; and we need not doubt that, when Horace writes of the "Lesbian lyre" handed to him by the Muse (*Odes* I, 1, lines 33-34), he is thinking primarily of his literary kinship with Alcaeus. The same is true of the Lesbian plectrum with which Horace hopes to immortalize Lucius Lamia (*Odes* I, 26, lines 10-12.).

In view of such explicit references to Alcaeus as these we have been examining, it is not surprising to find in the *Odes* clear examples of literary imitation. And we can be sure that, if

the full Alcaean corpus were extant, there would be many more
examples than those we are about to survey. We may begin the
survey by glancing at a theme which Horace has derived simultaneously from Archilochus and Alcaeus. As L. P. Wilkinson
observes, "The shield that he [Horace] admits [in the third
stanza of *Odes* II, 7] with scarcely a blush ... to have left on the
field of Philippi, had been left in a bush by Archilochus, and
before the walls of Sigeum by Alcaeus."[33] The very slight remains
of the Alcaean poem and the summaries of its content by
Herodotus and Strabo indicate that Horace's imitation of Alcaeus
in this instance is thematic rather than verbal. The same may be
said of the third stanza of *Odes* I, 10, which derived its reference to the theft by Mercury of Apollo's cattle and quiver from
Alcaeus's Hymn to Hermes.[34] In the case of Alcaeus's "Lady of
Misery" (A 10) and the twelfth *Ode* in Horace's third Book, the
fragmented state of Alcaeus's poem makes it impossible to specify
the exact nature of the imitation, if indeed it exists at all. The
only thing that can be said with assurance is that both poems are
composed in the same meter.[35] There are, however, sure instances
of verbal imitation of Alcaeus by Horace, and we may now
appropriately turn to these.

Striking examples of verbal imitation are afforded by Horace's
famous Ship of State poem (*Odes* I, 14), whose allegorical theme,
too, is inspired by Alcaeus's nautical allegories. In Horace's
allegory a ship foundering in a storm and being torn apart by
wind and wave is exhorted by the poet to make for port before
it is too late. As was indicated in antiquity by the critic Quintilian,
Horace's ship stands for the Roman Republic, while the storm
and the harbor symbolize respectively civil war and peace.[36] A
major difference between the Horatian and the Alcaean allegory
is that Alcaeus's storm-racked ship is a Ship of Party, whereas
Horace's represents the State as a whole. Nevertheless, verbal
imitations connect Horace's Ode with two of Alcaeus's allegories,
"The Ship: I" (A 6) and "The Ship: II" (Z 2). Alcaeus's reference to another wave about to strike his ship ("The Ship: I,"
lines 1-2) finds expression in Horace's additional waves (*novi
fluctus*), which will drive his Ship of State back out to sea (lines
1-2), just as Alcaeus's "and to a secure harbor let us run" ("The
Ship: I," line 8) is echoed in Horace's "start making/ For harbor,
run in hard" (lines 2-3). Also, Alcaeus's description of a tattered

sail with great rents in it ("The Ship: II," lines 7-8) is reflected in the Horatian phrase "Your sails are torn" (line 9).

Successive translations will give the reader an idea of Horace's extensive verbal and profound thematic debt to Alcaeus's "Winter" (Z 14) in the first two stanzas of *Odes* I, 9.[37]

> Zeus rumbles and a mammoth winter of snow
> pours from the sky; agile rivers are ice.
>
> Damn the winter cold! Pile up the burning logs
> and water the great flagons of red wine;
> ("Winter," lines 1-7)

> Look how the snow lies deeply on glittering
> Socracte. White woods groan and protestingly
> Let fall their branch-loads. Bitter frost has
> Paralysed rivers: the ice is solid.
>
> Unfreeze the cold! Pile plenty of logs in the
> Fireplace! And you, dear friend Thaliarchus, come,
> Bring out the Sabine wine-jar four years
> Old and be generous....
> (*Odes* I, 9, lines 1-8)

Again, Alcaeus's "And don't raise any other plant before the vine" (Z 18) is freely rendered by Horace at *Odes* I, 18, 1 into "Give the sacred vine the preference, Varus, when you plant your trees" (*Nullam, Vare, sacra vite prius severis arborem*). And "Today is the day to drink" (*nunc est bibendum*), with which Horace begins his Ode proclaiming the death of Cleopatra (I, 37), loosely translates Alcaeus's "Myrsilus Is Dead!" (Z 8): "Now's the time to get drunk and with some vigor/ to drink, for Myrsilus has died, indeed he has..." Here, as elsewhere, Horace's use of Alcaeus is more kinetic than substantive; for Horace's Cleopatra has replaced Alcaeus's Myrsilus, and after his Ode's Alcaean beginning Horace develops his theme in a quite independent and Roman manner.

In the last, and in *all* instances of Alcaean imitation by Horace, Alcaeus's verses function as a literary catalyst, which stimulates a process of lyric creation that is, in the last analysis, uniquely Horace's own. A lesser poet would have lacked both the skill and the inspiration to imitate so creatively. But imitation, and the tribute implied therein, by a lesser poet would have conferred on Alcaeus a lesser distinction.

PART III

The Poet as Metrician

CHAPTER 9

Greek Metrics and the Alcaic Stanza

I English Metrics

IN English the meters of poetry are determined by accent, so that a line of poetry is composed metrically of a series of stressed and unstressed syllables; and the arrangement of the components in this series goes far toward determining the rhythm of the verse.[1] (I use rhythm as a comprehensive term including meter and all that bears upon the effects of meter.) If we mark each relatively unstressed syllable with (.) and each prominently stressed syllable with (/), we would scan A. E. Housman's short poem, "With rue my heart is laden," in the following manner. (Words of more than one syllable will be scanned according to their dictionary accentuation, monosyllables according to the amount of stress they receive within their immediate context.)

. / . / . / .
With rue my heart is laden,
. / . / . /
For golden friends I had,
. / . / . / .
For many a rose-lipt maiden
. / . / . /
And many a lightfoot lad.
. / . / . / .
By brooks too broad for leaping
. / . / . /
The lightfoot boys are laid;
. / . / . / .
The rose-lipt girls are sleeping
. / . / . /
In fields where roses fade.

Although there is an extra unstressed syllable at the end of the first and third lines in each stanza, the basic metrical unit is the iamb (. /); and the rhythm of the two stanzas is similar. There is, however, a striking rhythmical variation, when one compares the last two verses of stanza 1 with the same verses in stanza 2. The lighter, more rapid rhythm of the former pair of verses (in contrast to the slower, more somber rhythm of the latter pair) is achieved by the substitution after the first iamb in each verse of an anapest (. . /) for the second iamb. In general terms, the rhythm of the poem is indicated by the arrangement of stressed and unstressed syllables.

II *Greek Metrics*

It is true that some syllables in English are longer than others. For example, *fate* takes longer to pronounce than *fat,* and in the first line of Housman's poem the unstressed "with" takes longer to pronounce than the similarly unstressed "is" or the final syllable of "laden." Nevertheless, as is quite clear from the scansion of Housman's poem, syllable quantity is not a determining factor in metrical analysis.[2] (And by syllable quantity I mean the amount of time required to pronounce a given syllable.) The situation is quite different with ancient Greek poetry, in which word accent has nothing to do with metrical structure and the meters must be analyzed in terms of syllable quantity; that is, in terms of longs and shorts, since every syllable can be classified as either long or short, whether it receives a word accent or not. This is not to claim that every short or every long requires the same amount of time to pronounce as all other shorts and longs. It is simply to state that every Greek syllable can be classified as long or short—and according to clearly defined rules at that—and that the rhythms of poetry are largely based upon an arrangement of longs and shorts in a pattern selected by the poet. This quantitative principle applies to the poems of Alcaeus as well as to all other ancient Greek poetry. (I am not here concerned with modern Greek poetry, which employs accentual meters similar to what we are accustomed to in English; and in this and the next chapter all references to Greek poetry will apply only to its ancient, classical form.)[3]

The reader will need some general knowledge of the rules governing Greek metrics, if he is to acquire an understanding of the meters employed by Alcaeus; and my next task will be to set forth these rules and then illustrate them by application. Since meter is based on syllable quantity, it is necessary to know what determines quantity before one can scan a line of Greek poetry, and the basic rules may be summarized as follows. (For the sake of any Greekless readers who have ventured into these somewhat technical chapters, all Greek letters will appear in transliterated form.)

1. In Greek all vowels are classified as either long or short, and a syllable is long if it contains a long vowel.

Table of Long Vowels[4]

Vowel	Transliteration Used in This Book	Suggested Pronunciation
Long alpha	ā	as the first *a* in English *drama*
Eta, a long *e*	ē	as the *e* in *they*
Long iota	ī	as the second *i* in *intrigue*
Long upsilon	ū[5]	as the *ew* in *few*
Omega, a long *o*	ō	as the *o* in *ocean*

2. A syllable is long if it contains a diphthong. A diphthong is a combination of two vowels which are pronounced as a single unit and which, therefore, are not to be assigned to separate syllables. For purposes of syllablic division a diphthong has the same function as a vowel.

Table of Diphthongs

Diphthong	Transliteration Used in This Book	Suggested Pronunciation
Alpha + iota	ai	as the *ai* in English *aisle*
Epsilon + iota	ei	as the *ei* in *freight*
Omicron + iota	oi	as the *oi* in *toil*
Upsilon + iota	ui	as *we*
Alpha + upsilon	au	as *ow* in *cow*
Epsilon + upsilon	eu	as a rapid *eh* ‿ *oo*
Eta + upsilon	ēu	as a rapid *ēh* *oo*

Omicron + upsilon	ou	as the *ou* in *group*
Long alpha + iota	āi	as long alpha (see the Table of Long Vowels above), since the *i* is silent.
Eta + iota	ēi	as eta (see the Table of Long Vowels above), since the *i* is silent.
Omega + iota	ōi	as omega (see the Table of Long Vowels above), since the *i* is silent.

The last three entries in this list are known as "improper diphthongs." They are frequently printed with an "iota subscript"—that is, with the iota under its accompanying vowel. In the transliterations used in this book, however, the *i* will be placed on the line beside the other vowel.

3. A syllable is short if it contains a short vowel, unless that short vowel is followed by two or more consonants, in which case the syllable is long. A short vowel so lengthened is said to be long by position.

Table of Short Vowels

Vowel	Transliteration Used in This Book	Suggested Pronunciation
Alpha	a	as the final *a* in English *drama*
Epsilon, a short *e*	e	as the *e* in *epic*
Iota	i	as the *i* in *if*
Omicron, a short *o*	o	as the *o* in *obey*
Upsilon	u	as the *ew* in *few*, but more rapidly

With regard to length by position, each of the double consonants zeta, xi, and psi (which will be transliterated respectively as *z*, *ks*, and *ps*) functions as two consonants and lengthens a preceding short vowel. Phi, theta, and chi (which will be transliterated respectively as *ph*, *th*, and *ch*) do *not* function as double consonants and, therefore, will not lengthen a preceding short vowel. It should also be noted that the two consonants need not, though they frequently do, occur in the same word. For example, the last syllable of a word ending in a short vowel followed by a single consonant (e.g., *hippos*) is to be scanned long if the next word begins with a consonant (e.g., *hippōs tis*). Also, a final short vowel not followed in its own word by a consonant is long if the next word begins with two consonants or a double consonant. For example, in the phrase *ana straton* the final vowel of *ana*, though short by nature, becomes long in this particular phrase because *straton* begins with two consonants.

What actually happens in the case of length by position is that the two consonants work together to close the preceding syllable, so that the amount of time required to pronounce it is increased: for example, in *hip-pos* the short *i* is lengthened when its syllable is closed by the first of the two succeeding consonants. The same thing happens to the short *a* of *aksios*. On the other hand, a *single* consonant between two vowels goes with the following vowel, so that if the preceding vowel is short by nature it remains short in scansion, since its syllable is not closed and, therefore, not lengthened. For example, in *philos* the short *i* is to be scanned short since the *l* is pronounced with the following syllable.

4. The last syllable of every verse of poetry is to be regarded as long, even if it would otherwise be scanned as short—that is, even if it contains a short vowel not followed by either two consonants or a double consonant.[6] According to this rule the last word in line 1 of Alcaeus's "The Ship: II" (Z 2) should be scanned *stasis,* although the *i* is naturally short.

Many would regard the final syllable of such a verse as a *syllaba anceps,* a syllable of indifferent quantity that is to be scanned as either long or short according to the rules just outlined. I would prefer to treat it as a syllable that must always be scanned as long because of the pause at the end of its verse, and I would classify every final short as a *syllaba brevis in elemento longo* (usually shortened to *brevis in longo*), a short syllable automatically lengthened by its position at the end of a line.[7]

III   *The Alcaic Stanza*

As I indicated at the beginning of this chapter, and as the rules which have just been set forth should confirm, the metrical basis of poetry in ancient Greek is fundamentally different from what it is in English. It is one thing to build meters on syllable stress (and unstress), as Housman did in "With rue my heart is laden," but quite another thing to build them on syllable quantity. Let us now analyze metrically some verses in both Greek and English for purposes of illustration and comparison. Since the subject of this book is Alcaeus, it seems appropriate to center this analysis on a verse form frequently used by him; and I have selected the one named after him, the Alcaic stanza.

In setting forth the Greek version of this stanza the following symbols will be employed: —, one long syllable; ◡, one short syllable; x, one syllable that may be either long or short. (According to rule 4 above, every short syllable at the end of a verse should be classified as a *brevis in longo* and scanned as a long, because of the pause at the end of the verse. For the present, however, it will be convenient not to distinguish between a true *anceps* and a *brevis in longo*. In the following metrical scheme every syllable that may be long or short, for whatever reoson, will be indicated by an x.)

Greek Version of the Alcaic Stanza

$$x - \cup - x - \cup \cup - \cup x$$
$$x - \cup - x - \cup \cup - \cup x$$
$$x - \cup - x - \cup - x$$
$$- \cup \cup - \cup \cup - \cup - x$$

I will soon analyze the two fully preserved stanzas of "The Ship: II" (Z 2) in terms of this metrical scheme, but a few preliminary explanations may prove helpful. These stanzas will be printed in transliterated form rather than in the Greek alphabet, so that the Greekless reader, if he so desires, will be able to pronounce them with the aid of the tables of vowels and diphthongs previously given. (Consonants may be pronounced as they would be in English. It is for this reason that I have not included a table detailing their pronunciation.) Lest the Greekless reader rebel at the thought of pronouncing something that is incomprehensible to him, let me point out that metrical knowledge can be acquired without an understanding of the language itself. It is certainly true that such knowledge will lack the depth that it would have if it were coordinated with the ability to comprehend the meaning of the verses to which it is being applied and that it will obviously never enable one to appreciate the subtle relation between rhythm and content. It will, however, make possible the development of some feeling for the rhythms employed by the ancient poet and, what is perhaps more important, of an understanding of what is involved when a Greek metrical scheme is adapted to English poetry. In other words, metrics is a science that may be studied apart from anything else, and on the preceding pages I have attempted to formulate the basic rules with which the study of Greek metrics must begin. To them should be added the fact that rhyme in the modern sense of the word is unknown to ancient Greek poetry and is to be categorically excluded from its study.[8]

The following marks and signs will be printed along with the transliterated text of the two stanzas. First, vowels naturally long will be printed with a dash (-) immediately over them; and both diphthongs and short vowels, even if the latter are long by position, will have no such marking. Secondly, the Greek word accents, which are three in number (acute [′], grave [`], and circumflex [Λ]), will be included, so that the reader can see for himself that word stress in Greek has nothing to do with the meter. In the case of an accented diphthong, the mark will be placed over the second member of the combination (e.g., aí, eì, oû). Thirdly, the following scansion marks will be employed: (⌣) for short syllables and (−) for long syllables. These scansion marks will be placed well above each syllable and are not to be confused with either the accent or the long vowel marks. A scansion mark will appear over every syllable, but the other two types of marks will occur only with certain syllables. Fourthly, I will use the system of punctuation that is now universally employed in printing ancient Greek. The comma and the period will have the same function as in English, and a raised dot (·) will be equivalent to an English semicolon. Finally, the syllables of verses 1 and 4 of stanza 1 will be numbered solely for the purposes of the following metrical commentary, whose goal is to give the reader some selective guidance in applying the abstract form of the Alcaic stanza to a particular stanza. It is hoped that after examining these two verses with the aid of the commentary he will be able to analyze the other verses for himself.

"The Ship: II" (Z 2), Stanza 1

1 2 3 4 5 6 7 8 9 10 11

∪ _ ∪_ ∪ _ ∪∪ _   ∪∪
     ´   `   ´   ´
asunnetēmmi tōn anemōn stasin

∪ _ ∪ _ _ _ ∪ ∪_ ∪_
`  ` ` ´   ^   ´
to men gar enthen kūma kulindetai,

∪ _ ∪ _ _ _ ∪ _ ∪
`  ´    ´    ` ` ´
to d'enthen, ammes d'on to messon

1 2 3 4   5 6 7   8 9 10
_∪ ∪ _   ∪∪ _   ∪ _ _
^   ´   `   ´
nāï phorēmmetha sun melainai

Metrical Commentary to Stanza 1
(The reference numbers are to syllables.)

Verse 1

1: The syllable is scanned as short since its vowel is naturally short and is not followed by two consonants. The poet could have used a long syllable here, as he does in this position in stanza 2, since the stanza form he is employing shows an *anceps* as the first syllable in each of the first three verses.

2: Scanned as long since its vowel, though short, is followed by two consonants. Alcaeus had to place a long syllable here, since that is what his metrical scheme demanded.

3: Scanned as short, since its short vowel is not followed by two consonants. Note that in this instance the word accent falls on a short syllable.

4: Scanned as long both because its vowel is long and because this vowel is followed by two consonants.

5: Scanned as short because its short vowel is not followed by two consonants. Since this syllable is an *anceps* in the stanza form, Alcaeus could have placed a long syllable here.

6: Scanned as long because its vowel is long. Here word accent happens to coincide with length.

7 and 8: Both scanned as short because each has a short vowel not followed by two consonants.

9: Scanned as long, since its vowel is long both by nature and by position.

10 and 11: Both scanned as short, since each contains a short vowel not lengthened by position. Syllable 11 could have been scanned long and is in fact lengthened by the pause at the end of the verse.

Verse 4

1 and 2: Two syllables, not an improper diphthong (see the last three entries in the Table of Diphthongs above). The diaeresis (¨) over the *i* indicates that in this particular instance the *a* and *i* belong to separate syllables and are to be pronounced accordingly. The first syllable (*nā*) is scanned long because its vowel is naturally long. The second (*i*) is short and is so scanned, since *ph* is a single consonant in Greek (phi) and does not, therefore, lengthen a preceding short vowel as a double consonant would.

5: Scanned as short since it is naturally short and *th* is a single consonant in Greek (theta).

7: The *u* is long by position. Note that the two consonants occur in different words.

9 and 10: Both scanned as long because each contains the diphthong *ai*.

Stanza 2

$$- \; - \; \cup \; - \quad - \; - \; \cup \; \cup \; - \; \cup \; \cup$$

cheimōni mochthentes megalōi mala.

$$- \; - \; \cup \; - \; \cup \; - \; \cup \; \cup \; - \; \cup \; -$$

per men gar antlos istopedān echei,

$$- \; - \; \cup \; - \; \cup \; - \; \cup \; - \; -$$

laiphos de pan zadēlon ēdē,

$$- \; \cup \; \cup \; - \; \cup \; \cup \; - \; \cup \; - \; \cup$$

kai lakides megalai kat auto,

The poet writing in Alcaics has a choice with regard to the initial syllable in each of the first three verses. (The first syllable of the fourth verse is not an *anceps* and must be long.) Alcaeus has chosen three initial shorts for stanza 1 and three longs for stanza 2. This consistency of choice, however, was not demanded by his stanza form, and he might have used any possible combination of longs and shorts for his initial *ancipites* (plural of *anceps*). In fact, in each stanza his treatment of syllable 5 in verses 1-3 (it is an *anceps*) reveals variety of choice. Also, a more extensive selection of diphthongs appears in stanza 2. In addition to the *ai* of the first stanza, there is *ei* (in *cheimōni*, verse 1 and *echei*, verse 2) and *au* (in *auto*, verse 4).

If a reader should ask how it is possible for metrical structure to be divorced from word accent and for this accent not to lengthen the syllable on which it falls, I would have to reply that I do not know, but that the evidence provided by all ancient Greek poetry establishes beyond a shadow of a doubt that it is so. I would add, however, that I am not claiming that rhythm (which I use here, just as I did at the beginning of this chapter with reference to English poetry, as a comprehensive term including meter and all that bears upon the effects of meter) is not affected by word accent. Indeed, it must have been. It is merely that, in contrast to English poetry with its stress rhythms, the fundamental rhythm of a verse or stanza of Greek poetry is determined by a meter based on syllable quantity and that only secondary modifications are introduced by such elements as word accent and word color.[9] In answer to this same question I would also caution against assuming that the principles of English metrics are universally applicable to all languages. Indeed, the testimony of Greek poetry proves that they are not. And I would add that one of the basic lessons to be learned from the study of the literature—and, indeed, the whole culture— of another people is that ours is not the only way of doing something. The differences, of course, tend to become more marked as the other culture is more remote from ours in time or heritage, or, as in the case of ancient Hellas, in both.

IV *Lattimore and the Alcaic Stanza*

The adaptation of a Greek metrical scheme to fit the requirements of English versification is, therefore, a largely artificial process, even in those instances when the English poet is experimenting and attempting to write quantitative rather than stress poetry. For to subject the English language to the rules of quantitative metrics that govern Greek poetry is to impose on it strictures which it is not linguistically equipped to bear, and to adapt the Greek meter by equating long syllables with stressed syllables and short syllables with unstressed syllables is to destroy the quantitative foundation of the original, Greek rhythm. By pointing this out I do not intend to decry the adaptive process or to censure its results, for it has justified itself by spawning much fine poetry in English. My purpose is solely to establish its nature, not evaluate the outcome.

We will presently examine a quantitative adaptation of the Alcaic stanza by Tennyson; but I would first like to offer a metrical analysis of Richmond Lattimore's translation of the two Alcaeus stanzas that were recently quoted. Lattimore has attempted a stress adaptation of the Alcaic stanza, equating original longs and shorts respectively with English stresses and unstresses.[10] Since both the fact and the nature of the metrical adaptation are certain, Lattimore's stanzas may be scanned with confidence. Because Lattimore's meter is based on word accent rather than syllable quantity, I will employ the same scansion marks used previously for Housman's poem. (A stressed syllable will be marked with [/] and an unstressed one with [·].) The reader can judge for himself the success of the modern poet's adaptation. (Certain syllables will be numbered for the purposes of the following metrical comments.)

```
1            5                        11
·  /  ·  /  ·  /   ·    ·  /   ·  /
I cannot understand how the winds are set

1              5                      11
·  /  ·   /  ·  /   ·    ·  /   ·   /
against each other. Now from this side and now

      1              5        9
      ·  /  ·   /   /  /   ·   /
      from that the waves roll. We between them

                                      10
      /  ·  ·   /   ·   /   ·   /   ·
      run with the wind in our black ship driven,

1              5                      11
/   /   ·   /  ·   /   ·    ·  /  ·   /
hard pressed and laboring under the giant storm.
```

1   5   11

/ / . / . / . . / . /

All round the mast-step washes the sea we shipped.

1   5   9

. / .   /   . / . / .

You can see through the sail already

                           10

/ . . / . . /   . / .

where there are opening rents within it.

Metrical Comments

1. The numbered syllables in each stanza are those occurring where the original Alcaic form of this meter offers a syllable that may be either long or short. Lattimore has adapted by employing variously and to suit his convenience stresses and unstresses at these points.

2. Because of our awareness of the metrical scheme being used by Lattimore, we know to scan and pronounce *laboring* (stanza 2, verse 1) with two syllables (as *lab'ring*).

3. Lattimore is struggling against the fact that even for Greek poetry the Alcaic stanza is metrically a highly rigid form, while English poetry tends toward more metrical license and a freer use of metrical substitutions and modifications. This fact asserts

                    / . . /

itself emphatically in the phrases "Now from this side" (stanza

            . / . /

1, verse 2) and "You can see through" (stanza 2, verse 3), whose scansion is dictated by the Alcaic original but which only under duress fits into the required metrical pattern.

4. The basic differences between quantitative and stress metrics are apparent throughout the translation. For example, the "in" of stanza 1, verse 4 and the *in* that constitutes the final syllable of "within" (stanza 2, verse 4) each require the same amount of absolute time for pronunciation, yet the former is unstressed while the latter is stressed; and the unstressed first syllable of "within" takes as long to pronounce as the stressed second syllable. Also, the stressed "where" and the unstressed "there" of stanza 2, verse 4 have the same absolute length. In each of these examples it is on the basis of the presence or absence of stress that the syllable contributes to the rhythm of its verse, and the syllable's quantity is of no more than secondary impor-

tance. The converse is true of the original, quantitative metrical scheme which Lattimore is adapting.

V *The Recitation of Greek Poetry*

The principles of Greek metrics we can formulate, and, despite some uncertainties in particular areas or instances, we can confidently apply these principles to the scansion of any body of poetry. It is when we attempt to translate these principles into oral recitation that we become most keenly aware of the limits of our knowledge. The amount of pure guesswork and arbitrary decision-making involved in setting up any rules for reading Greek poetry aloud is enough to cause the beginner to despair at the first syllable. Many, however, have found that even the most erroneous system, as long as it is consistent, has increased their appreciation of Greek poetry; and I would like to outline the several systems of oral recitation that an English-speaking person may employ. Before doing this it is necessary to call attention to a factor that both complicates the situation and at the same time may be responsible for the fact that the principles of Greek metrics can be outlined apart from those of word accent. It is that in ancient Greek accent was not a matter of stress, as it is in English, but of pitch: the three accent marks (the acute ´ , the grave ` , and the circumflex ^) thus indicate three different *tones* or *pitches* of the voice rather than any kind of stress. And there is a sharp and clear distinction between these musical accents, which indicate elevation and depression of tone, and metrical quantity, which involves only duration of tone.[11]

A system of oral recitation consistent with our knowledge of Greek accent and rhythm would employ some sort of a chant that recognizes both change of tone and duration of tone. The latter would be taken into account by assigning approximately the time of two short syllables to one long; and the former would necessitate a raising of pitch at syllables accented with the acute, a lowering at those with the grave, and a raising followed by a lowering at those with the circumflex. It should be noted that the circumflex itself (^) is a combination of an acute (´) and a grave (`) and that it may fall only on long vowels or diphthongs, both of which must, therefore, be composed of two tonal units, in contrast to short vowels, which may receive only the acute or the grave and so offer a single tonal unit.

The system of recitation just outlined, though the most accurate, is at the same time the most complex and the most difficult to master, particularly for the unmusical ear.[12] There are, however, two other systems frequently used, which, if not as consistent with ancient practices, still can gratify the yearning to read poetry aloud and can convey some sense of the rhythm of the original. One is a compromise between Greek and English practices. There is no attempt to bring out the tonal qualities originally indicated by the Greek accents; and all accented syllables receive an English stress, no matter whether the accent mark is acute, grave, or circumflex. This is a concession to English pronunciation. At the same time the quantitative principle underlying Greek metrics receives its due; for longs are read long and shorts short, with each long being allotted approximately the same amount of time as two shorts. The main difficulty in this system arises when an accent falls on a syllable that is metrically short, since it is no easy task for an English speaking person to stress a syllable without increasing the amount of time required for pronunciation.

However, even the most unmusical among us, in which number I count myself, need not despair, for there is a perfectly acceptable system of oral recitation that disregards Greek metrical principles and allows us to recite Greek poetry as we would English. Word accent is completely ignored and a stress called an *ictus* is placed on designated syllables, in most cases long syllables. By this system the Alcaic stanza is read with an *ictus* or stress on each syllable that is invariably long, all other syllables remaining unstressed; and for recitation with *ictus* it may be diagrammed as follows. (The *ictus* will properly be designated by /, the same symbol used to indicate stress in scanning English poetry.)

$$x\ \overset{/}{-}\ \cup\ \overset{/}{-}\ x\ \overset{/}{-}\ \cup\ \cup\ \overset{/}{-}\ \cup\ x$$

$$x\ \overset{/}{-}\ \cup\ \overset{/}{-}\ x\ \overset{/}{-}\ \cup\ \cup\ \overset{/}{-}\ \cup\ x$$

$$x\ \overset{/}{-}\ \cup\ \overset{/}{-}\ x\ \overset{/}{-}\ \cup\ \overset{/}{-}\ x$$

$$\overset{/}{-}\ \cup\ \cup\ \overset{/}{-}\ \cup\ \cup\ \overset{/}{-}\ \cup\ \overset{/}{-}\ x$$

If we employ this system, we should bear in mind that there was no such thing as an *ictus* in ancient Greek poetry and that we resort to the *ictus* merely as a means of reciting something whose tones and rhythms we cannot accurately reproduce—in short, that our system, though adequate for our purposes, is nevertheless completely artificial.[13]

VI *Tennyson and the Alcaic Stanza*

The reader may gain some feeling for the rhythmical structure of the Alcaic stanza by reading aloud with close attention to syllable quantity Alfred Lord Tennyson's *Milton,* subtitled "Alcaics" and by its author's express indication written according to the principles of quantitative metrics. In fact, in his notes to this poem Tennyson goes so far as to contrast the Alcaics of Alcaeus with those of his Latin imitator Horace and to insist that the rhythmical structure of *Milton* is after the manner of the Greek rather than the Latin poet.[14] I will quote and scan Tennyson's entire poem, appropriately employing the scansion marks of quantitative metrics and relying on Tennyson's metrical notes for the scansion of several syllables. Extrapolations from these notes will be explained in the metrical comments following the poem:[15]

<pre>
_ _ ∪ _   _ _ ∪ ∪ _ ∪ _
O mighty-mouth'd inventor of harmonies,

_   _ _   ∪   _ _   _   ∪ ∪ _ ∪ ∪
O skill'd to sing of Time or Eternity,

     _   _ ∪ _   _   _   ∪ _ _
   God-gifted organ voice of England,

      _ ∪ ∪ _   ∪ ∪ _   ∪ _ ∪
   Milton, a name to resound for ages;   4

   _   _ ∪ _ _   _ ∪∪ _ ∪ ∪
Whose Titan angels, Gabriel, Abdiel,

  _   _   ∪ _ _   _ ∪∪ _ ∪ _
Starr'd from Jehovah's gorgeous armouries,

      _   _   ∪ _   _   _ ∪_∪
   Tower, as the deep-domed empyrëan

     _   ∪ ∪ _ ∪ ∪ _ ∪ _ ∪
   Rings to the roar of an angel onset—   8

  _   _ ∪ _   _   _∪∪ _ ∪ _
Me rather all that bowery loneliness,
</pre>

The brooks of Eden mazily murmuring,

And bloom profuse and cedar arches

Charm, as a wanderer out in ocean,   12

Where some refulgent sunset of India

Streams o'er a rich ambrosial ocean isle,

And crimson-hued the stately palm-woods

Whisper in odorous heights of even.   16

Metrical Comments

1. In keeping with the principles of quantitative metrics and the intent of the author, I have scanned as long all syllables that may be viewed as having a long vowel or diphthong: for example, O (line 1), *Time* (line 2), *voice* (line 3), *domed* (line 7), *out* (line 12), the first syllable of *even* (line 16). I have also scanned as long all syllables which would be classified as long by position according to the rules of Greek metrics—that is, whose vowel is followed by two or more consonants. In his notes Tennyson himself remarks two otherwise short syllables that he regards as long by position: the final syllable of *organ* (line 3, before *voice*) and *the* (line 15, before *stately*). And his son and editor, Hallam Lord Tennyson, calls attention to two other such syllables: *from* (line 6, before *Jehovah's*) and *as* (line 7, before *the*). I have, therefore, scanned as long all syllables that offer a vowel followed by more than one consonant: for example, the first syllable of *inventor* (line 1), *of* (line 2, before *Time*), the final syllable of *angels* (line 5), and every *and* (lines 11 and 15). No exception is made in the case of *thē* before *brooks* (line 10), since in Alcaeus the special combination of a mute (here *b*) followed by a liquid (here *r*) regularly functions as two consonants and, therefore, metrically lengthens a preceding short vowel.[16] Though this fact could not have been surely known in Tennyson's day, his assertion that *the* before *st-* (line 15) is long and his conscious striving to imitate Alcaeus rather than Horace show that he would have approved my scansion of *the* as long before *br-*.

2. All syllables that could not reasonably be classified as long

by applying the rules of quantitative metrics outlined earlier in this chapter have been scanned as short.

3. Four problems of pronunciation are resolved by the rigid demands of the Alcaic stanza for a specific number of syllables in each line. Tennyson himself points out that *Milton* (line 4) must be pronounced with two full syllables and not as *Milt'n*. Likewise *gorgeous* (line 6) must be pronounced and scanned as a trisyllable and *ambrosial* (line 14) as a quadrisyllable. Conversely, *Tower* (line 7) must be treated as a monosyllable.

Not only has Tennyson written in unrhymed verse, as was demanded by his Greek model; throughout the poem, as I have attempted to demonstrate by my scansion and metrical comments, he has adhered as closely to the metrical scheme of the Alcaic stanza and to the practices of quantitative metrics as the English language would permit. *Milton* is, of course, still very much an English poem. For one thing, there is a strong tendency in English for accent to lengthen the syllable on which it falls, so that in a quantitative poem like *Milton* metrical length and word stress coincide to a far higher degree than in Greek poetry. Nevertheless, it is impossible to fully appreciate the rhythm of *Milton* or to read it aloud as its author would have it read without an understanding of both the Alcaic stanza and the quantitative metrical principles which Tennyson is employing.

CHAPTER 10

The Meters of Alcaeus

I The Nature of Metrical Theory

THE science of metrics, when applied to ancient Greek poetry, is largely a matter of convention and convenience. We have almost no knowledge of the metrical theories and concepts of Alcaeus and the other poets of classical Greece; and whatever metrical theorizing has survived from antiquity is generally fragmentary and has proved quite inadequate for the analysis of Greek poetry.[1] Modern students of Greek metrics have, therefore, tended to take over the metrical terminology of the ancients but to use it for developing and explaining their own theories about the meters and rhythms employed by the original poets. These theories have been worked out independently of those of the ancients and are the ones that form the basis of contemporary metrical criticism of Greek poetry. Thus, the only true tests of any current theory are its usefulness and its meaningfulness, its usefulness for the systematic classification of meters and metrical practices, and its meaningfulness for the appreciation of the rhythmical qualities of the poetry. The understanding and explanation of metrical phenomena are the absolute most that the metrician can hope to achieve; for, as was just indicated, metrical information from antiquity is sorely limited. We have no idea as to how Alcaeus himself would have organized and presented a description of the metrical phenomena in his own poetry, but we can be sure that his description would have differed, perhaps radically, from ours. At the same time, we can also be sure that we have an amazingly precise knowledge of these phenomena and of Alcaeus's metrical practices, especially in view of the fact that his poetry has survived in only fragmentary form and was written over 2,500 years ago. The point is, the metrical practices *can* be understood—and this is the really important thing—even if our description of them differs from that which Alcaeus would have offered. If we aim exclusively at understanding and judge metrical theories solely on the basis of usefulness and meaningfulness, we can achieve a high degree of appreciation of the meters that undergird the rhythms of Greek poetry.

II *The Aeolic Meters*

"Aeolic" is the term used to designate the lyric meters most closely associated with Alcaeus and Sappho and in which the bulk of their extant poetry was composed. To judge from the surviving fragments, only occasionally did Alcaeus venture beyond the rather narrow confines of the Aeolic meters, for in only eight of the approximately 125 fragments whose metrical nature is identifiable is there evidence that he was employing a "non-Aeolic" metrical scheme.[2] Present consideration will, therefore, be limited to the meters in which Alcaeus composed the vast majority of his poetry—and to these meters as they were employed by Alcaeus. What is said about the Aeolic metrics of Alcaeus will necessarily apply to those of Sappho, for their practices in this area are fundamentally the same. No attention, however, will be paid to the Aeolic meters as they were utilized by later poets, whose metrical practices often diverged from those of Sappho and Alcaeus.

In the United States the most easily accessible and commonly followed explanations of the Aeolic meters are those of Denys Page in his book *Sappho and Alcaeus* and of Thomas G. Rosenmeyer in *The Meters of Greek and Latin Poetry*.[3] These two explanations, though not contradictory, are certainly different and will not yield to synthesis. This is a fact which is often not appreciated,[4] and my immediate purpose is to describe and compare Page's and Rosenmeyer's systems of metrical analysis. Page's system is based on an essay by A. M. Dale entitled "The Metrical Units of Greek Lyric Verse," and Rosenmeyer's is derived from Bruno Snell's *Griechische Metrik*.[5] For the sake of convenience I will frequently designate the advocates of the two systems simply as S-R (for Snell and Rosenmeyer) and as D-P (for Dale and Page); and minor departures by the disciple from the author of the system will be ignored, unless they impinge on matters of principle.

Before turning to these systems, three observations about Sappho's and Alcaeus's Aeolic meters may be made which are, on the basis of available evidence, universally true and irrespective of a given system of metrical analysis. First, perhaps the most distinctive feature of these meters is that two shorts may not be substituted for a long nor a long for two shorts, so that the number of syllables in a metrical scheme may not vary. This feature is driven home if we compare a verse in the so-called Aeolic dactyls with a dactylic hexameter of the Homeric type. Because of substitution the number of syllables in a Homeric hexameter may theoretically vary from twelve to seventeen

($\_ \overline{\cup\cup}$ $\_ \overline{\cup\cup}$ $\_ \overline{\cup\cup}$ $\_ \overline{\cup\cup}$ $\_ \overline{\cup\cup} \_ \_$); but the number of syllables in a line of Aeolic dactyls is rigidly fixed at fourteen (x x $\_ \cup\cup$ $\_ \cup\cup$ $\_ \cup\cup$ $\_ \cup \_$), since no such substitutions are allowed. Secondly, within a given type of verse the position of every *anceps*—that is, every syllable that may be long or short at the poet's discretion—is invariable. For example, the first verse of the Alcaic stanza always exhibits *ancipites* (pl. of *anceps*) in the first and fifth positions and at no other point: x $\_ \cup \_$ x $\_ \cup \cup \_ \cup \_$. In other words, the responson of a long to a short and vice versa is permitted, but only under carefully regulated and clearly definable circumstances. Thirdly, the combination of a mute (pi, beta, phi, tau, delta, theta, kappa, gamma or chi) followed by a liquid (lambda, rho, mu, or nu) always functions as two separate consonants and, therefore, lengthens a preceding short vowel: for example, the first syllable of *pet-ros*, whose naturally short epsilon (*e*) is followed by the mute tau (*t*) plus the liquid rho (*r*), would invariably be scanned as long in the metrical contexts under consideration. This in effect means that *every* combination of two consonants lengthens a preceding short vowel.

III *Snell and Rosenmeyer's System of Metrical Analysis*

Let us now turn to S-R's system. Its fundamental feature is that all the Aeolic meters are analyzed in terms of the glyconic (diagram: x x $\_ \cup \cup \_ \cup \_$, symbol: *gl*) and the iambic metron (diagram: x $\_ \cup \_$, symbol: *ia*). And I will carry the implication of this to its logical conclusion and eliminate from my explanatory vocabulary several traditional terms retained by Snell: pherecratean (x x $\_ \cup \cup \_ \_$) and hipponactean (x x $\_ \cup \cup \_ \cup \_ \_$), which are variations of the glyconic;

also cretic (– ◡ –) and bacchiac (◡ – –), which are
variations of the iambic metron. In addition, the terms "line"
or "verse" will be used comprehensively to include S-R's
"period."[6] I will thus simplify S-R's vocabulary in the belief
that basic metrical patterns are only obscured by proliferation of
descriptive vocabulary. This simplification has made it necessary
for me to alter some of the marginal symbols employed by S-R
to designate the metrical units of Aeolic verse. For instance,
they designate a hypermetric glyconic as a "hipponactean" and
use the symbol *hipp* to identify this unit. I have employed the
symbol *gl+*. The set of symbols is basically theirs, however, and
I have introduced alterations only where necessary. I have, of
course, followed S-R in treating the final syllable of every verse
as a long; for if it would otherwise be short, it functions in their
system as a *brevis in longo* (a short syllable automatically
lengthened by the pause at the end of the line).

The glyconic consists of two *ancipites* (frequently referred
to as its "Aeolic base") followed by six syllables in a prescribed
sequence: x x – ◡ ◡ – ◡ –. However, it is possible by
catalexis (the *omission* of a final syllable) to produce a catalectic
glyconic (diagram: x x – ◡ ◡ – –, symbol: *gl*Λ) and by the
addition of a final syllable to produce a hypermetric glyconic
(diagram: x x – ◡ ◡ – ◡ – –, symbol: *gl+*). (The final
syllable of both the catalectic and the hypermetric glyconic is
diagrammed as long because it always constitutes a verse end.)
In addition, *acephaly* (the *omission* of an initial syllable) may
be applied to each of these three units (the pure glyconic,
the catalectic glyconic, and the hypermetric glyconic), so that
it is possible to have an acephalous glyconic (diagram: x – ◡
◡ – ◡ –, symbol: Λ*gl*), an acephalous catalectic glyconic (diagram: x – ◡ ◡ – –, symbol: Λ*gl*Λ), and an acephalous hypermetric glyconic (diagram: x – ◡ ◡ – ◡ – –, symbol: Λ*gl+*).
In all, the Aeolic poet had at his disposal six basic metrical units
composed of the pure glyconic and its five variations.

Although each of these basic units may constitute a complete
verse, a line of Aeolic poetry usually consists of one of these
units combined with something else. This combining is called
"compounding," and the compounding may be either external
or internal. I will describe the two types of compounding
separately.

External compounding may involve no more than the joining together of two or even three of the basic units. Its most common form, however, is the addition of an iambic metron to the beginning or the end of a basic unit. Moreover, this iambic metron has a full and a shortened form. The full form consists of two iambs, and its first syllable is an *anceps*: x − ◡ − (symbol: *ia*). This form may either precede or follow the basic unit. The shortened form appears initially as an acephalous iambic metron (diagram: − ◡ −, symbol: Λ*ia*) and finally as a catalectic iambic metron (diagram: ◡ − −, symbol: *ia*Λ). (Since the catalectic iambic metron always forms a verse end, its final syllable is diagrammed as long.) To illustrate external compounding we may take the first verse of the Alcaic stanza (x − ◡ − x − ◡ ◡ − ◡ −), which is to be analyzed as a full iambic metron (x − ◡ −) plus an acephalous glyconic (x − ◡ ◡ − ◡ −). Its symbol is *ia*, Λ*gl*. Similarly, the first line of the Sapphic stanza (− ◡ − x − ◡ ◡ − ◡ − −) is to be viewed as an acephalous iambic metron (− ◡ −) plus an acephalous hypermetric glyconic (x − ◡ ◡ − ◡ − −). Its symbol is Λ*ia*, Λ*gl*+.

Internal compounding is produced by the insertion of dactyls (− ◡ ◡) or choriambs (− ◡ ◡ −) into a glyconic or one of its five variations. For example, a line of Aeolic dactyls is properly to be analyzed as a pure glyconic compounded internally by two dactyls: x x − ◡ ◡ [− ◡ ◡ − ◡ ◡] − ◡ −. Its symbol is *gl* [2d]. Likewise an asclepiadean is to be explained as a pure glyconic compounded internally by the insertion of a single choriamb: x x − ◡ ◡ − [− ◡ ◡ −] ◡ −. Its symbol is *gl*[c]. When compounding internally the poet must choose between the dactyl and the choriamb, since they may not appear simultaneously within the same basic unit.

I would like to illustrate more fully the system of metrical analysis just outlined by applying it to the Alcaic and Sapphic stanzas, two of the most influential creations of Aeolic metrics and both commonly employed by Alcaeus.

Metrical Scheme of the Alcaic Stanza
after Snell and Rosenmeyer

1. x − ◡ −, x − ◡ ◡ − ◡ − *ia*, Λ*gl*
2. x − ◡ −, x − ◡ ◡ − ◡ − *ia*, Λ*gl*
3. x − ◡ −, x − ◡ −, x − ◡ ◡ [− ◡ ◡] − ◡ − − 2 *ia*, Λ*gl*[d]+

According to S-R this is a three verse rather than a four verse stanza. Traditionally, their third verse has been printed as two separate lines, with the break occurring after the ninth syllable; and it was the traditional form in which the stanza was presented in the preceding chapter. S-R's theoretical conviction, however, that the glyconic (or one of its variations) must occur in every verse of Aeolic poetry makes it impossible to separate the third verse into two separate lines, for to do so would be to produce two lines without a glyconic in either. The fourth verse would not contain a glyconic because of the loss of the Aeolic base (the initial anceps of $\Lambda gl^{d}+$) to the preceding line, and the third verse would exhibit an unexplainable extra syllable attached to the end of two iambic metra.

Not all the evidence, however, is theoretical, and there are considerable factual data which indicate that S-R have given a reasonable and cogent metrical analysis of the last verse of the Alcaic stanza. First, Alcaeus *never* in any of his extant poetry in this stanza form allows hiatus between the traditional third and fourth lines. (Hiatus is a situation in which a word ending in a vowel is followed by a word beginning with a vowel. It is a strong indication of verse end.) Secondly, "The Reef" (D 15), which uses the Alcaic stanza form, offers an example of elision between the third and fourth verses of its second stanza. (Elision is a situation in which a word ending in a vowel or diphthong loses this final vowel or diphthong before a word beginning with a vowel. It is a strong indication of the absence of verse end.) Thirdly and most importantly, Alcaeus has left two certain instances where a single word overlaps from the third to the fourth lines (D 17, line 13 and K 5 [a] ii, lines 4-5).

Metrical Scheme of the Sapphic Stanza
After Snell and Rosenmeyer

1. — ∪ —, x — ∪ ∪ — ∪ — — Λ*ia*, Λgl+
2. — ∪ —, x — ∪ ∪ — ∪ — — Λ*ia*, Λgl+
3. — ∪ —, x — ∪ ∪ — ∪ —, x — ∪ ∪ — — Λ*ia*, Λgl, $\Lambda gl\Lambda$

Again, S-R's third verse has traditionally been printed as two lines, with the break after the eleventh syllable:

3. — ∪ — x — ∪ ∪ — ∪ — x
4. — ∪ ∪ — x

And again, S-R's glyconic theory dictates that such a division is impossible, for it leaves the fourth line without a glyconic. Also, Sappho's practice with this stanza form emphatically militates against separating S-R's third verse into two lines; for she avoids hiatus and commonly allows word overlap between traditional lines 3 and 4. One of many examples of word overlap is provided by the first stanza of her famous *Phainetai moi* poem (no. 31 in the edition of Lobel and Page), the poem that was adapted by the Latin poet Catullus (no. 51 in editions of Catullus). Since the Sapphic stanza was also favored by Alcaeus, I will illustrate the practical application of S-R's theory by applying it to the first stanza of this particular poem. The traditional fourth line will be set apart so as to reveal the word overlap.

$$- \cup -, \; - \; - \cup \cup - \; \cup - -$$

1. phaínetai moi kênos ísos theoisin $\Lambda ia, \; \Lambda gl +$

$$- \; \cup \; -,- \; - \cup \cup - \cup - \; -$$

2. emmen' ōnēr, ottis enántios toi $\Lambda ia, \; \Lambda gl +$

$$- \cup -, \; - \; - \cup \cup - \cup \; -,- \; - \cup \cup - -$$

3. ísdanei kai plásion ādu phōnei—sās upakouei $\Lambda ia, \; \Lambda gl, \; \Lambda gl \Lambda$

Alcaeus employs a number of stanza and verse forms in addition to the Alcaic and Sapphic stanzas. So that the reader may gain some further idea of the organization of his Aeolic metrical patterns, I will diagram and symbolize according to S-R's system those of the other forms that can be identified with reasonable certainty. Whenever there are traditional names for these forms, they will be given; and an example of each form will be cited at the beginning of its entry. This list, however, does not reveal the full number of Aeolic metrical forms employed by Alcaeus; for there are additional forms which cannot be accurately classified because of the exceedingly fragmentary nature of the lines and stanzas by which they are attested.

Aeolic Verse Forms

A. Minor asclepiadean (Z 27)

  $x \, x - \cup \cup - [- \cup \cup -] \cup - \quad gl^c$

B. Major asclepiadean (Z 22)

x x – ∪ ∪ – [– ∪ ∪ – – ∪ ∪ –] ∪ – gl^{2c}

C. x x – ∪ ∪ – [– ∪ ∪ – – ∪ ∪ – – ∪ ∪ –] ∪ – gl^{3c} (Z 64)

D. Aeolic dactyls (Z 41)

x x – ∪ ∪ [– ∪ ∪ – ∪ ∪] – ∪ – gl^{2d}

E. x x – ∪ ∪ [– ∪ ∪ – ∪ ∪ – ∪ ∪] – – $gl{\Lambda}^{3d}$ (Z 45)

F. [7] x x – ∪ ∪ – ∪ –, x x – ∪ ∪ – ∪ –, x – ∪ – 2 *gl, ia* (Z 34)

Aeolic Stanza Forms

A. x x – ∪ ∪ – [– ∪ ∪ –] ∪ – gl^c (G 2)
  x x – ∪ ∪ – [– ∪ ∪ –] ∪ – gl^c
  x x – ∪ ∪ – ∪ – – $gl+$
  x – ∪ ∪ – [– ∪ ∪ –] ∪ – Λgl^c

B. x – ∪ –, x x – ∪ ∪ – ∪ –   *ia, gl* (D 12)
  x x – ∪ ∪ – [– ∪ ∪ –] ∪ – gl^c

C. [8] x x – ∪ ∪ – [– ∪ ∪ –] ∪ – gl^c (A 5, D 9)
  x x – ∪ ∪ – [– ∪ ∪ –] ∪ – gl^c
  x x – ∪ ∪ – [– ∪ ∪ –] ∪ – gl^c
  x x – ∪ ∪ – ∪ – *gl*

IV *Dale and Page's System of Metrical Analysis*

Let us now turn from Snell and Rosenmeyer's system of metrical analysis to that advocated by Dale and Page, bearing firmly in mind that we are still dealing with the same body of literature, the poems of Alcaeus (and, by implication, of Sappho as well). It is not the rhythms that will change, only the system of analyzing and describing them. According to D-P there are two basic units in the lyric poetry of Alcaeus as in *all* lyric poetry: the cretic (diagram: – ∪ –, symbol: *s* because it contains a *single* short between two longs) and the choriamb (diagram: – ∪ ∪ –, symbol: *d* because it contains a *double* short between two longs). Either of these units may be preceded or followed by an *anceps* or both, and they are used to form various rhythms by means of prolongation and addition.

These two phenomena will soon be described separately, but first a few preliminary items. Page's concept of terminal syncopation will be disregarded as an unnecessary and ambiguous refinement of Dale's theory. For example, Page classifies the traditional

fourth line of the Sapphic stanza (− ∪ ∪ − ≃) as a syncopated version of − ∪ ∪ − ∪ − and diagrams it as − ∪ ∪ − −
                                                                                                ∪
or − ∪ ∪ − (Λ) −, indicating with his terminology and diagrams that a short between two longs has dropped out by metrical syncopation and that a final short in this line is to be classified as a *brevis in longo*.[9] Dale, however, classifies this line as − ∪ ∪ − ≃ (that is, as a choriamb plus an *anceps*) and would diagram it as d≃. In all such circumstances I will follow Dale rather than Page. (I would, however, designate the *anceps* by x instead of ≃, and would diagram the line as − ∪ ∪ − x and symbolize it as *dx*. I will, in fact, continue to represent the *anceps* by x throughout my presentation of D-P's system.) In addition, it should be pointed out that although Page endorses Dale's theory he does not employ her *s* and *d* symbols—or for that matter any symbols at all. For instance, she symbolizes − ∪ ∪ − ∪ − as *ds*, while Page refers to it only as the "element − ∪ ∪ − ∪ −." Likewise, Dale more or less successfully eschews such traditional terms as "cretic" and "choriamb," which are freely used by Page. I will combine these two terms with Dale's symbolism in my description of D-P's system.

To return to prolongation and addition. In the case of the former, one of the basic metrical units (that is, a cretic or a choriamb) shares its final long with the initial long of a following cretic or choriamb; and the prolongation my include several, not just two, of the basic units. The prolongation of a choriamb by a cretic is particularly common (diagram: − ∪ ∪ − ∪ −, symbol: *ds*); and the traditional fourth line of an Alcaic stanza (diagram: − ∪ ∪ − ∪ ∪ − ∪ − x, symbol: *ddsx*) is to be regarded as having a choriamb prolonged by another choriamb, with the second choriamb in turn prolonged by a cretic and with an *anceps* attached to the end of the entire prolongation.

In the case of addition, basic units, in either simple or prolonged form are joined together without sharing a common long. Frequently an *anceps* is placed between the constituent units. In Dale's symbolism addition without *anceps* is indicated by a short vertical line between the symbols for the basic units: e.g., − ∪ ∪ − − ∪ ∪ − is symbolized by *d|d*. Addition with *anceps* is marked by the simple presence of the *anceps* sign: for instance, x − ∪ − x − ∪ − has as its composite symbol *xsxs*. An asclepiadean (diagram: x x − ∪ ∪ − − ∪ ∪ − ∪ −, symbol: *xxd|ds*) is, according to D-P's system, produced by addition: two *ancipites* plus a choriamb plus a choriamb-cretic prolongation. We observe an intervening *anceps* in the first verse of the Alcaic stanza (diagram: x – ∪ – x – ∪ ∪ – ∪ –, symbol: *xsxds*), which is to be described additively as *anceps* plus cretic plus *anceps* plus choriamb-cretic prolongation.

The same body of Alcaic metrical patterns previously analyzed according to S-R's system will now be subjected to D-P's system. The latter offers no theoretical reasons for combining the traditional third and fourth lines of the Alcaic and Sapphic stanzas into a single verse. Factual data, however, are invariable, and the same data that persuasively argued for such combining under S-R's system apply equally to D-P's. Only three lines, therefore, will be assigned to these stanza forms in the following list:

Aeolic Verse Forms

A. Minor asclepiadean (Z 27)
x x – ∪ ∪ – | – ∪ ∪ – ∪ –   *xxd|ds*

B. Major asclepiaden (Z 22)
x x – ∪ ∪ – | – ∪ ∪ – | – ∪ ∪ – ∪ –   *xxd|d|ds*

C. x x – ∪ ∪ – | – ∪ ∪ – | – ∪ ∪ – | – ∪ ∪ – ∪ – *xxd|d|d|ds* (Z 64)

D. Aeolic dactyls (Z 41)
x x – ∪ ∪ – ∪ ∪ – ∪ ∪ – ∪ –   *xxddds*

E. x x – ∪ ∪ – ∪ ∪ – ∪ ∪ – ∪ ∪ – x   *xxddddx* (Z 45)

F. [10]x x – ∪ ∪ – ∪ – x x – ∪ ∪ – ∪ – x – ∪ –   *xxdsxxdsxs* (Z 34)

Aeolic Stanza Forms

A. The Alcaic Stanza (Z 2)
x – ∪ – x – ∪ ∪ – ∪ –   *xsxds*
x – ∪ – x – ∪ ∪ – ∪ –   *xsxds*
x – ∪ – x – ∪ – x – ∪ ∪ – ∪ ∪ – ∪ – x   *xsxsxddsx*

B. The Sapphic Stanza (B 2. a)
– ∪ – x – ∪ ∪ – ∪ – x   *sxdsx*
– ∪ – x – ∪ ∪ – ∪ – x   *sxdsx*
– ∪ – x – ∪ ∪ – ∪ – x – ∪ ∪ – x   *sxdsxdx*

C. xx – ∪ ∪ – | – ∪ ∪ – ∪ –   *xxd|ds* (G 2)
xx – ∪ ∪ – | – ∪ ∪ – ∪ –   *xxd|ds*
xx – ∪ ∪ – ∪ – x *xxdsx*
x – ∪ ∪ – | – ∪ ∪ – ∪ –   *xd|ds*

D.   x – ∪ – x x – ∪ ∪ – ∪ –   *xsxxds* (D 12)
     xx – ∪ ∪ – | – ∪ ∪ – ∪ –   *xxd|ds*

E. ¹¹xx – ∪ ∪ – | – ∪ ∪ – ∪ –   *xxd|ds* (A 5, D 9)
     xx – ∪ ∪ – | – ∪ ∪ – ∪ –   *xxd|ds*
     xx – ∪ ∪ – | – ∪ ∪ – ∪ –   *xxd|ds*
     xx – ∪ ∪ – ∪ –   *xxds*

V   *A Comparison*

Such in outline are two different systems for describing and classifying the Aeolic meters of Alcaeus (and of Sappho). For Snell and Rosenmeyer the basic fact of these meters is the "glyconic" (and I am here using the term comprehensively to include its five modified forms). It may be compounded by other units; but it is still possible to view all of Alcaeus's Aeolic meters—in other words, the meters of nearly all of his surviving poetry—as variations on the glyconic, since every verse written in them exhibits a glyconic nucleus. For Dale and Page, however, the basic units of the same body of meters are the cretic and the choriamb, which Alcaeus is always in the process of prolonging and, with the aid of the *anceps*, adding together. Because we know absolutely nothing about Alcaeus's own metrical theory, it would be incorrect to characterize one system as right and the other as wrong, or even to claim that they are contradictory in the literal sense of the word. Nevertheless, it is apparent that they are quite different—and mutually exclusive. By this I mean that, although one may analyze a given verse by one system and then analyze it again by the other system, it is not possible to make a synthesis of the two systems and employ them simultaneously. All this does not mean, however, that the two systems may not or should not be evaluated and compared as to meaningfulness and usefulness. In conclusion to this chapter I will essay such an evaluation and comparison.

From an exclusively personal and pedagogical point of view, I would say that D-P's system is the simpler of the two—but so simple as to be amorphous, particularly when applied to a metrically varied body of poetry. S-R's system, though more complex and more difficult to comprehend in theoretical form, offers more order and security when finally grasped and actually applied to lines of Greek verse.

But this is not the whole story, for there is one comparative evaluation that may be expounded with somewhat more objectivity. It has to do with the double *anceps* that occurs internally (for example, in the first line of the stanza form used by Alcaeus in "Pittacus" [D 12]: x − ∪ − x x − ∪ ∪ − ∪ −) as well as initially (for example, in an asclepiadean: x x − ∪ ∪ − − ∪ ∪ − ∪ −) in certain types of Aeolic verses. D-P's system makes no allowance for this double *anceps*; and, when it occurs, they are forced to recognize it in their diagrams and symbols simply because it occurs, not because it was taken into account from the beginning and integrated into their metrical theory and symbolism. The double *anceps* in effect protrudes inexplicably when it appears in verses being analyzed after D-P. S-R, on the other hand, incorporate the double *anceps* into their theory by taking the glyconic as the fundamental metrical unit in each verse; for in their system every double *anceps* functions as the Aeolic base of some form of glyconic, and the single *anceps* of the various acephalous glyconics is viewed as a deliberately halved version of its double form, which now no longer appears as a metrical prodigy.

Another functional advantage to S-R's glyconic as against D-P's cretic-choriamb system is that the former enables us to classify the meters of Alcaeus's and Sappho's lyric poetry as either "Aeolic" or "non-Aeolic."[12] (I am here referring *only* to meter, not dialect; and I, of course, exclude the dozen or so of Sappho's dactylic hexameters that have survived. Their meter is epic, not lyric, and as such is to be analyzed and classified separately by the same system that is applied to Homeric poetry. No dactylic hexameters of the Homeric type by Alcaeus have survived, and there is no evidence that he ever employed this meter.) The overwhelming majority of Alcaeus's and Sappho's lyric meters exhibit a glyconic unit, and these may be classified by S-R's system as purely "Aeolic," while the remaining minority, which do not contain this basic unit, may be grouped together under the rubric "non-Aeolic" and subjected to appropriate sub-classification. It is absolutely impossible by D-P's system to make a classification of this sort, or, indeed, to analyze the lyric meters employed by Sappho and Alcaeus in any but the most general way.

Alcaeus Z 60 may be cited to illustrate the point I am making.

_ ∪∪ _ ∪ ∪ _ _   _ ∪ _ _

ḕr' eti Dinnomenē tō Turrakḗō

_ ∪∪ _ ∪ ∪ _   _   _ ∪ _ _

tarmena lampra keont' en Mursinḗōi;

The metrical responsion of the two lines is precise throughout, and they are immediately recognizable as dactylo-epitrites of a very common variety. As such they exhibit no glyconic unit and by S-R's system may be segregated from the bulk of Alcaeus's poetry as non-Aeolic in metrical structure. By D-P's theory, however, these dactylo-epitrites, which are so reminiscent of choral lyric and so strikingly different from the meters customarily employed by Alcaeus and Sappho, must be regarded as fashioned in the same metrical crucible that produced their glyconic verses; for by D-P's system, each of these two verses is easily symbolized as *ddxsx* and just as easily analyzed as a double-choriamb prolongation plus an *anceps* plus a cretic plus an *anceps*.

In my opinion, there are definite advantages to employing systems of metrical analysis that enable us to divide the Greek lyric meters into manageable and reasonably classified groups. These advantages become more compelling when one turns from the relatively strict and simple metrical patterns used by Alcaeus and Sappho to the exceedingly complex and heterogeneous combinations of choral lyric, whose very complexity is attributable to the fact that a given poet, frequently in a given ode, draws from and combines a variety of metrical types and traditions. Snell and Rosenmeyer have propounded a system of metrical analysis whereby one can distinguish and isolate what is distinctively "Aeolic" not only in the poems of Alcaeus and Sappho but also in, say, the odes of Pindar or a dramatic chorus.

Notes and References

Chapter One

1. Burn's *The Lyric Age of Greece* (London, 1960) is a masterful account of the history, literature, and thought of the Greek world in the seventh and sixth centuries B. C.

2. On the nature of Greek lyric poetry see, e.g., C. M. Bowra, *Greek Lyric Poetry* (Oxford, 1961), pp. 1-15 and, more briefly, Richmond Lattimore (tr.), *Greek Lyrics* (Chicago and London, 1960), pp. iii-vi.

3. The papyrus copies were made during the first three centuries of our era (see Edgar Lobel and Denys Page, *Poetarum Lesbiorum Fragmenta* [Oxford, 1955], pp. x-xi). The dates of the manuscripts containing the quotations by later writers, though they vary, are much later. For a brief history of the Alcaeus papyrus finds, see in Pauly-Wissowa, Supplementband XI (1968), coll. 8-10 Max Treu's supplement to Crusius's 1893 Alcaeus article.

4. For accounts of the Greek migrations to the eastern Aegean and the coast of Asia Minor, see J. B. Bury, *A History of Greece*, third edn. rev. by Russell Meiggs (London, 1952), pp. 63-73; J. M. Cook, *Greek Settlement in the Eastern Aegean and Asia Minor* (Cambridge, 1961); and N. G. L. Hammond, *A History of Greece* (Oxford, 1967), pp. 82-88. Cook's work is the fascicle that will eventually constitute Ch. XXXVIII in Vol. II of the new ed. of The Cambridge Ancient History.

5. These allegories will be discussed at length in Ch. 4.

6. On the date for the introduction of coinage, see C. M. Kraay, *Greek Coins* (London, 1966), pp. 11-12 and Hammond (above, note 4), pp. 131-34.

7. For a summary of this evidence, see Burn (above, note 1), pp. 145-46.

8. Herodotus II, 178-79. The archaelogical and literary evidence on the Greek settlement at Naucratis is assembled and discussed by R. M. Cook, "Amasis and the Greeks in Egypt," *The Journal of Hellenic Studies*, LVII (1937), 227-37. See also John Boardman, *The Greeks Overseas* (Baltimore, 1964), pp. 134-50.

9. On the Charaxus-Rhodopis affair and Sappho's reaction to it, see Herodotus II, 134-35; the Sapphic Fragments 5 and 15 (b) in Lobel-Page; and, for translation, comment, and interpretation, Denys Page, *Sappho and Alcaeus* (Oxford, 1955), pp. 45-51.

10. Our information about this peasant class is best for Attica. See W. J. Woodhouse, *Solon the Liberator* (Oxford, 1938).

11. For a concise, readable history of Greek tyranny, see A. Andrewes, *The Greek Tyrants* (New York and Evanston, 1963). Andrewes describes its Mytilenean expression on pp. 92-99, as does Page (above, note 9), in much greater detail and in conjunction with the Alcaean corpus, on pp. 149-243. On tyranny at Mytilene see also Helmut Berve, *Die Tyrannis bei den Griechen* (Munich, 1967), I, 91-95 and II, 572-75.

12. For this chronology see Diogenes Laertius I, 75 and 79 and Page (above, note 9), p. 151.

13. Diogenes Laertius I, 74-75 and Aristotle, *Politics,* 1285ᵃ 29-40.

14. Diogenes Laertius I, 76 and Diodorus Siculus IX, 12, 3.

Chapter Two

1. See D 12, line 6 and the comments by Denys Page, *Sappho and Alcaeus* (Oxford, 1955), p. 236 and by Max Treu, *Alkaios* (Munich, 1963), p. 164.

2. Diogenes Laertius I, 74 and the Suidas, s.v. *Pittakos.*

3. The scholia occur at line 23 of E 1, line 8 of M 8 (a), and line 19 of R 1. For the content of these scholia see Lobel and Page's *apparatus criticus.*

4. For these scholia see, in addition to Lobel and Page's *apparatus,* Page (above, note 1), p. 180.

5. See E. Lobel (ed.), *The Oxyrhynchus Papyri,* vol. XXXV (London, 1968), pp. 1-2.

6. Cf. the parallels pointed out by Lobel (above, note 5), p. 6 (in connection with papyrus 2734, Fragment 6).

7. Richmond Lattimore (tr.), *Greek Lyrics* (Chicago and London, 1960), pp. 42-43 and Page (above, note 1), p. 183. For a metrical analysis of Lattimore's translation, see Chapter 9 of this book.

8. For text and translation of Heraclitus's remarks (*Allegories,* Ch. 5), see J. M. Edmonds, *Lyra Graeca,* vol. 1 (London and New York, 1922), pp. 344-45; Page (above, note 1), p. 184, n. 1 and p. 188, n. 1; and esp. Félix Buffière's Budé edition of the *Allegories* (Paris, 1962), pp. 4-6. Despite the obvious (to a modern) fallacy of Heraclitus's Homeric exegesis, there is absolutely no reason to doubt the basic correctness of his allegorical interpretation of the poetry he discusses in Ch. 5.

9. Aristotle, *Politics* 1285ᵃ 29-37.

10. Diogenes Laertius I, 74. Cf. Strabo XIII, 1, 38 and see Page (above, note 1), pp. 152-61.

11. The mythical founder of this clan was Penthilus, who was the son of Orestes. Orestes was the son of Agamemnon, who was in

turn the son of Atreus. Hence Alcaeus's reference to "the House of Atreus."

12. On all this as well as Pittacus's laws and reputation see Aristotle, *Politics* 1274[b] 18-23; Diogenes Laertius I, 75-78; Strabo XIII, 2, 3; and A. Andrewes, *The Greek Tyrants* (New York and Evanston, 1963), pp. 96-99.

13. On Alcaeus and Pittacus see Carl Theander, "De Alcaei Poematis in Hyrrhan, Pittacum, Penthilidas Invectivis," *Aegyptus*, XXXII (1952), 179-90 and Page (above, note 1), pp. 152-79 and 235-43. Theander focuses his article on D 14, A 5, D 17, and F 5.

14. On Pittacus as *kakopatridas* see Page (above, note 1), pp. 169-74 and P. Odo Bauer, "Sapphos Verbannung," *Gymnasium*, LXX (1963), 1-10. Pittacus was base-born in no ordinary sense of the word; and both Page and Bauer argue that in applying this epithet to him Alcaeus was attacking the foreign (Thracian: see Diogenes Laertius I, 74), though aristocratic, origin of his father. Bauer believes that, in addition to Pittacus, Alcaeus regarded Myrsilus and even Sappho as base-born in the sense that they too belonged to an immigrant nobility.

15. This translation is by Richmond Lattimore, *The Iliad of Homer* (Chicago and London, 1961), p. 82.

16. For fuller discussion of this image of Pittacus see Ch. 5 and note 11.

17. Denys Page, *The Oxyrhynchus Papyri*, vol. XXIX (London, 1963), pp. 17 and 42-43.

18. For exhaustive discussion of D 14 and its problems, see Page (above, note 1), pp. 171-74.

19. On the origin of Pittacus's father see Diogenes Laertius I, 74 and note 14, above.

20. A 5 is not discussed in Page's *Sappho and Alcaeus*. On Pittacus as the subject of this poem see Treu (above, note 1), pp. 164-65.

21. The poem in question is described in Fragment 77 (lines 16-32) of papyrus number 2506 in the Oxyrhynchus collection. For text and discussion of Fragment 77, see Page (above, note 17), pp. 17 and 42-43 and W. Barner, "Zu den Alkaios-Fragmenten von P. OXY. 2506," *Hermes*, XCV (1967), 1-15.

22. On Pittacus's appointment as *tyrannos* and his clemency toward Alcaeus, see respectively Aristotle, *Politics* 1285[a] 35-37 and Diogenes Laertius I, 76.

23. My translation "force our way" is based on Page (above, note 1), p. 227 (note on *es polin elthēn*). "If haply we can" is derived from two facts of Greek grammar: Alcaeus's *dynāmetha* at D 11, line 3 is subjunctive (cf. *dynātai* at L 1, line 7), and in Homer the subjunctive is often introduced by *ai* (or *ei*) *ke* in the sense of "if

haply," "in the hope that" (e.g., at *Iliad* I, lines 66-67; I, line 207; and II, line 72).

24. A scholion to D 11 indicates that these misfortunes are those of Alcaeus's faction (see Lobel and Page's *apparatus*), but the scholiast may be doing no more than expressing his own opinion.

25. On the purchasing power of two thousand staters see Page (above, note 1), p. 232.

26. For the text and interpretation of these fragments, see Page (above, note 17), pp. 21-22 and 44-45 and Barner (above, note 21), pp. 15-28.

Chapter Three

1. For this and the two succeeding quotations, see A. E. Housman's *Selected Prose*, ed. John Carter (Cambridge, 1961), pp. 172 and 187-88.

2. It is interesting that the verses of *Paradise Lost* quoted are an adaptation of a passage in Book I of the *Iliad* (lines 590-94), where Hephaestus describes how Zeus once hurled him off Mount Olympus.

3. E.g., *Iliad* I, line 141; II, line 300; *Odyssey* II, line 430; III, line 61. For the Homeric usage of this epithet, see the entry *melās* in R. J. Cunliffe, *A Lexicon of the Homeric Dialect* (Norman, Okla., 1963).

4. E.g., *Odyssey*, Book XI, line 245; Pindar, *Isthmian Odes*, 8 (7), line 48; Euripides, *Alcestis*, lines 177-78 and *Trojan Women*, line 501; *Greek Anthology*, Book VII, no. 324; Plutarch, *Lycurgus*, 15.

5. In Z 106 the noun *gaurēx* is defined by a verb literally appropriate to horses and meaning "to prance." See *gauriaō* in Liddell and Scott's *Greek-English Lexicon*, rev. H. S. Jones and Roderick McKenzie (Oxford, 1940).

6. The Greeks normally drank a mixture containing more water than wine. See Denys Page, *Sappho and Alcaeus* (Oxford, 1955), p. 308.

7. For my interpretation of this fragment see Lobel and Page's *apparatus criticus* and Page (above, note 6), p. 295.

8. This is the explanation offered by Page (above, note 6), p. 172, n. 10.

9. On *agkyrrai* see Page (above, note 6), p. 187.

10. "Adornment" (*agalma*) is common in Homer (see Cunliffe [above, note 3]). On the epic connotations of "a defense against a powerful missle" see *Iliad* V, lines 315-16; IV, line 137; and Page (above, note 6), p. 214.

11. At Q 1, lines 25-26 the word for "sea" has been lost but is a sure conjecture. "Wine-dark" (*oinops*) normally modifies sea

(*pontos*) in Homer, and a word for "sea" is demanded by the context. For the ed. of Q 1 used by me, see below, Ch. 6, n. 4.

12. On "chilling" at D 3, line 14 see Lobel and Pages' *apparatus criticus*.

Chapter Four

1. On the motif of drinking in Alcaeus see Jürgen Trumpf, *Studien zur griechischen Lyrik* (diss. Cologne, 1958), pp. 8-31; C. M. Bowra, *Greek Lyric Poetry* (Oxford, 1961), pp. 157-62; Hermann Fränkel, *Dichtung und Philosophie des frühen Griechentums* (Munich, 1962), pp. 222-24; and Albin Lesky, *A History of Greek Literature*, trans. James Willis and Cornelis de Heer (London, 1966), p. 135.

2. On the "ritual of Greek drinking" as handled by Alcaeus, see Bowra (above, note 1), p. 158. Cf. Trumpf (above, note 1), pp. 19-24.

3. On the proportions of wine and water prescribed in this poem, see Denys Page, *Sappho and Alcaeus* (Oxford, 1955), p. 308.

4. On wine turning into vinegar see Page (above, note 3), p. 313.

5. On the meaning of *dioptron* (which I translate as "a window opening into") in Z 9, see Page (above, note 3), p. 312. Trumpf (above, note 1), p. 9 and Bowra (above, note 1), pp. 160-61 connect Z 43 and Z 9 very much as I do.

6. For bibliography on the question of allegory in Alcaeus's nautical images see Page (above, note 3), p. 182, n. 2.

7. See Page (above, note 3), pp. 181-82.

8. The following translation is by Richmond Lattimore, *The Iliad of Homer* (Chicago, 1951), p. 319.

9. The Archilochus fragment is no. 56 in Ernst Diehl's *Anthologia Lyrica Graeca*, fasc. 3 (Leipzig, 1952), p. 25; the ancient critic is the Heraclitus who will be discussed presently; and the translation is by Lattimore, *Greek Lyrics* (Chicago, 1960), p. 4.

10. In my interpretation of the Archilochean allegory I follow Page (above, note 3), pp. 181-82 and Fränkel (above, note 1), pp. 163 and 216, n. 4. On the possibility that the poem from which Archilochus's verses are quoted may have contained a ship allegory of the kind that will be suggested for Alcaeus, see Diehl (above, note 9), pp. 25-26, no. 56 A; Bowra (above, note 1), p. 152; and Lesky (above, note 1), p. 134.

11. For bibliography and examples see Page (above, note 3), p. 182, n. 1.

12. On Horace's debt to Alcaeus in *Odes* I, 14 see Giorgio Pasquali, *Orazio lirico* (Firenze, 1920), pp. 16-38; Page (above, note 3), pp. 183-84 and 187; Eduard Fraenkel, *Horace* (Oxford, 1957), pp.

154-58; Stelle Commager, *The Odes of Horace* (New Haven and London, 1962), pp. 163-69; L. P. Wilkinson, *Horace and His Lyric Poetry* (Cambridge, 1968), p. 72; and in Twayne's World Authors Series, Kenneth J. Reckford, *Horace* (New York, 1969), p. 71. Also, the Horace commentaries by E. C. Wickham (Vol. I [Oxford, 1904], pp. 35-36) and by Adolf Kiessling and Richard Heinze (Vol. I [Berlin, 1958], pp. 71-72). In this ode Horace was influenced by A 6 as well as by Z 2.

13. The formula Z 2 + V 1 ii + K 5 (a) ii designates "The Ship: II" as it is reconstructed by Page (above, note 3), pp. 185-88. Though I subscribe to this reconstruction, for the sake of convenience I will henceforth designate the poem simply as Z 2.

14. Heraclitus, *Allegories*, Ch. 5, pp. 4-6 in Félix Buffière's Budé edition (Paris, 1962). The Greek text of all the Heraclitus comments pertinent to the present chapter is given by Page (above, note 3), p. 184, n. 1 and p. 188, n. 1 and, together with an English translation, by J. M. Edmonds in his Loeb edition of Alcaeus (*Lyra Graeca*, vol. 1 [London and New York, 1922], pp. 344-45). On Heraclitus (often cited as Pseudo-Heraclitus), see Jean Pepin, *Mythe et Allégorie* (Aubier, 1958), pp. 159-67 and the Introduction to Buffière's Budé edition. Whatever the modern reader's reaction to Heraclitus's Homeric exegesis, there is absolutely no reason to question the fundamental correctness of his allegorical interpretation of the Alcaean and other poetry discussed in *Allegories*, Ch. 5.

15. The translation here offered of the first stanza of this poem is Page's (above, note 3), p. 19.

16. *Allegories*, Ch. 5, 8-9 (see above, note 14).

17. On this point see Page (above, note 3), pp. 184-85.

18. The commentator's remarks are listed in Lobel and Page's edition as X (14), column i. Page (above, note 3), pp. 191-96 regards column ii of X (14) as also part of the commentary on D 15. This leads him to an ingenious but fanciful interpretation of the poem. I follow G. L. Koniaris, "Some Thoughts on Alcaeus' Frs. D 15, X 14, X 16," *Hermes*, XCIV (1966), 385-97 in rejecting a connection between D 15 and X (14), column ii. At the same time, I think that Page has correctly related X (14), column i to D 15.

19. Cf. Koniaris (above, note 18), pp. 391 and 394.

20. On the possibility that X (14), column ii, is commenting on a poem in which a ship is symbolized as a prostitute or vice versa, see Page (above, note 3), pp. 191-96 and Koniaris (above, note 18), pp. 388-89. Cf. my note 18, above.

21. Cf. the judgment by Page (above, note 3), p. 196: "The advice in its literal meaning is commonplace in thought and expression, and we may do the poet less than justice if we do not admit

the likelihood that it is in fact not a maxim but a parable, addressed not to the mariner but to the politician."

22. On the comparison of Alcaeus's hymn with the other two, see Page (above, note 3), p. 267-68. On the date of the Homeric Hymn see also Page, p. 268 and n. 1 and A. S. F. Gow's commentary (*Theocritus*, vol. II [Cambridge, 1950]), p. 382 and n. 1. We are here concerned with only the first twenty-six lines of Theocritus's Idyll, its Prelude. The first volume of Gow's *Theocritus* (Cambridge, 1950) presents the Greek text of the Idylls with facing English translation.

23. On Saint Elmo's fire see Page (above, note 3), p. 267 and n. 2.

24. Indeed, Theocritus in his hymn to the Dioscuri describes a ship foundering in a storm (Idyll 22, lines 10-16).

25. For all Heraclitus passages discussed in this chapter, see my notes 14 and 16, above.

26. On this poem see Max Treu, *Alkaios* (Munich, 1952), pp. 183-85; Page (above, note 3), p. 242, n. 3; and Bowra (above, note 1), p. 171. Page describes its allegory as "the obscure parable of the vine" and suggests that it is political in reference.

Chapter Five

1. For the Greek text of the scholia pertinent to the interpretation of D 16, see Denys Page, *Sappho and Alcaeus* (Oxford, 1955), pp. 237-38.

2. For the Archilochean fragment, see Ernst Diehl, *Anthologia Lyrica Graeca*, fasc. 3 (Leipzig, 1952), p. 24.

3. On Z 70, see especially J. M. Edmonds, *Lyra Graeca*, v. I (London and New York, 1922), pp. 358-59; Carlo Gallavotti, *Saffo e Alceo*, v. II (Naples, 1957), pp. 41-42; and C. M. Bowra, *Greek Lyric Poetry* (Oxford, 1961), pp. 171-72.

4. For the interpretation of Z 112, see Edmonds (above, note 3), pp. 380-81 and Edgar Lobel and Denys Page, *Poetarum Lesbiorum Fragmenta* (Oxford, 1955), p. 289.

5. Bowra (above, note 3), p. 171.

6. On the interpretation of Z 28, see especially Edmonds (above, note 3), pp. 356-57 and A. S. F. Gow, *Theocritus*, v. II (Cambridge, 1950), pp. 122-23.

7. The source of Z 115 is Plutarch, *De defectu oraculorum* 410 B-C. Edmonds (above, note 3), pp. 360-61 gives Plutarch's Greek together with an English translation.

8. This translation is by Richmond Lattimore, *Greek Lyrics* (Chicago, 1960), p. 4.

9. This poem is no. 7 in Diehl's *Anthologia* (above, note 2), pp. 52-58.

10. For full discussion of this epithet (*lykaimiais*), see Page (above, note 1), pp. 205-6.

11. Because of the beast metaphor I translate the dative *posin* (line 22) as "with his paws" rather than "with his feet."

12. It is a question of whether the verb *phyiei* is active or intransitive. For the philological problems connected with this poem, see Page (above, note 1), pp. 291-93.

13. Lobel's theory is presented in *The Bodleian Quarterly Record*, III (1922), pp. 289-90. For a summary of it, see Page (above, note 1), pp. 292-93.

14. For examples, see *Iliad* III, lines 21-29; XI, lines 113-21; XI, lines 472-84; XIII, lines 99-106; XV, lines 271-78; XVI, lines 156-66; XVI, lines 756-61; XXII, lines 188-93; *Odyssey* IV, lines 335-40; and VI, lines 130-36.

15. The translation is by Lattimore, *The Iliad of Homer* (Chicago, 1961), p. 237.

16. On *bromos*, see Page (above, note 1), p. 292.

17. For Arrowsmith's translation, see *The Complete Greek Tragedies* (ed. David Grene and Richmond Lattimore), v. III (Chicago, 1959), p. 328.

18. There is no arguable reason for connecting A 10 and Z 57, as Page does (above, note 1), p. 291.

19. For the Homeric *pyrgos* (fortified wall) used figuratively of persons, see *Odyssey* XI, line 556; *Iliad* IV, line 334; IV, line 347; and XII, line 333.

Chapter Six

1. Denys Page, *Sappho and Alcaeus* (Oxford, 1955), p. 291.

2. My discussion of B 10 is based on the preserved text as it actually exists in Lobel and Page's edition. The treatment of the poem by Page (above, note 1), pp. 278-81 and by C. M. Bowra, *Greek Lyric Poetry* (Oxford, 1961), pp. 168-69 is somewhat misleading, since they are working from a text conjecturally restored to completeness by modern editors.

3. For my interpretation of B 12 and Z 31, see Page (above, note 1), pp. 281-83.

4. The short version of Q 1 which appears in Lobel and Page's *Poetarum Lesbiorum Fragmenta* (1955) has since been antiquated by the publication of a new and comparatively long papyrus fragment of this poem. The new fragment was published initially by Reinhold Merkelbach in *Zeitschrift für Papyrologie und Epigraphik*, I (1967), 81-82, and was utilized by Page in his *Lyrica Graeca Selecta* (Oxford, 1968), pp. 75-77. The definitive version of both Q 1 and the new fragment, however, is now that, with commentary

and discussion, by Hugh Lloyd-Jones, "The Cologne Fragment of Alcaeus," *Greek, Roman and Byzantine Studies,* IX (1968), 125-39. For the epic style of Q 1, see, in addition to Lloyd-Jones's article, Page (above, note 1), p. 285 and nn. 4-6.

5. On this fragment see Page (above, note 1), pp. 273-74. The Hesiod verse appears as Fragment 11 in A. Rzach's Teubner edition of Hesiod's *Carmina* (Leipzig, 1902), p. 134.

6. On M 4, see Page (above, note 1), p. 274, n. 3.

7. For my interpretation of A 7 and appropriate bibliography, see Page (above, note 1), p. 274, n. 3. The Greek text of the pertinent Pausanias remark is given both by Page (*loc. cit.*) and by Lobel and Page in the *apparatus criticus* to A 7.

8. Throughout my treatment of the Alcaean hymn, I am much indebted to Page (above, note 1), pp. 244-72 and 286-88, who is at his best on this particular subject.

9. The most pertinent ancient witnesses are Pseudo-Plutarch, *De Musica* 1135 F-1136 A; Pausanias X, 8, 10; and Himerius, *Orationes* XIV, 10-11. A Greek text of the Himerius passage is furnished by Page (above, note 1), p. 245, n. 1; and the Greek texts of all the sources are given by both Lobel and Page (item no. 307) and by Carlo Gallavotti, *Saffo e Alceo,* v. II (Naples, 1957), pp. 9-10.

10. The fragments and pertinent source material are grouped together as item no. 308 by Lobel and Page and as item no. 2 by Gallavotti (above, note 9), pp. 10-11. Page (above, note 1), p. 252, explains the word *gonai* in the phrase "*gonai* of Hephaestus and Hermes" (see item no. 308, 2 [a] in Lobel and Page's edition) as "the story of [a god's] birth and childhood."

11. My translation is designed to reflect the damaged state of the Greek text, which breaks off after the first word of verse four.

12. Page (above, note 1), pp. 255-58 argues this point with cogency.

13. As was true of both Ganymede and Hebe. In fact, the Greek form of Hebe, when not used as a proper noun, means "prime of youth" or "youthful beauty."

14. The fragments and pertinent source materials are grouped together as Z 25 by Lobel and Page and as item no. 41 by Gallavotti (above, note 9), pp. 26-27. Lobel and Page; Page (above, note 1), p. 259, no. 1; and Gallavotti (*loc. cit.*) all give the Greek text of Pseudo-Libanius, to whom I refer in my main text simply as a "late account" or "late authority." For an interpretation of the Z 25 fragments quite different from the one I will here present, see Bruno Snell, "Dionysos oder Hephaistos?," *Festschrift Ernst Kapp* (Hamburg, 1958), pp. 15-17. Snell argues that they derive from a Hymn to Dionysus rather than to Hephaestus.

15. For a list of the other accounts of this same story, see Page (above, note 1), p. 259, n. 1.

16. That these events occurred soon after Hephaestus's birth is evident from the sources listed by Page (above, note 1), p. 259, n. 1.

17. On this point see Page (above, note 1), p. 260. Lobel and Page list this fragment as Z 25 (b).

18. This fragment is listed as Z 25 (c) in Lobel and Page's edition, and is also assigned to the Hymn to Hephaestus by Gallavotti (above, note 9), p. 26.

19. For an ancient parallel, one may cite the textual tradition whereby at *Acts* I, 26, the eleven apostles remaining after the death of Judas are still referred to as "the twelve apostles." Many texts, including Nestle's, prefer the more precise tradition offering "eleven." R. V. G. Tasker, however, in his edition (Oxford and Cambridge, 1964) of the Greek text translated in *The New English Bible* offers "twelve," for which reading see the textual note to Acts I, 26 on p. 429.

20. The assignment is made by Gallavotti (above, note 9), p. 26, but not by Lobel and Page. Page's discussion of the evidence for the assignment (above, note 1), pp. 260-61 is marked by fairness and good sense.

21. Sappho's poem is the first item in Lobel and Page's *Poetarum Lesbiorum Fragmenta* (Oxford, 1955). For comment and translations, see, e.g., Page (above, note 1), pp. 3-18; Richmond Lattimore, *Greek Lyrics* (Chicago, 1960), pp. 38-39; and Willis Barnstone (trans.), *Sappho* (Garden City, 1965), pp. 26-27.

22. For detailed and cogent argumentation that the Hymns to Athena and Eros concern deities of local, Boeotian cults, see Page (above, note 1), pp. 268-72.

23. Plutarch's *Amatorius* is a masterful piece which transforms the local Eros of Thespiae into a universal god of love. See the translation of the *Amatorius* by W. C. Helmbold in the Loeb edition of Plutarch's *Moralia*, vol. IX (London and Cambridge, Mass., 1961), pp. 301-441.

24. On Eros's parentage, see Page (above, note 1), p. 271 and nn. 1-6.

25. See Page (above, note 1), p. 244.

26. E. Lobel (ed.), *The Oxyrhynchus Papyri*, vol. XXXV (London, 1968), pp. 2-4.

27. This classification was made long ago by J. M. Edmonds, *Lyra Graeca*, vol. I (London and New York, 1922), pp. 330-31.

Chapter Seven

1. For pertinent details about the Epic Cycle, see Richmond

Lattimore, *The Iliad of Homer* (Chicago and London, 1961), pp. 24-28.

2. See my discussion of Alcaeus's Hymns in the preceding chapter and Denys Page, *Sappho and Alcaeus* (Oxford, 1955), pp. 244-72.

3. For a concise, readable discussion of the oral composition of the Homeric poems, see G. S. Kirk, *Homer and the Epic* (Cambridge, 1965), pp. 1-32.

4. On the content of B 12, see Page (above, note 2), pp. 281-82.

5. The edition of Q 1 followed here and elsewhere is by Hugh Lloyd-Jones, "The Cologne Fragment of Alcaeus," *Greek, Roman and Byzantine Studies*, IX (1968), 125-39. For details about Q 1, see above, Ch. 6, n. 4. For the remains of the *Nostoi*, mentioned near the end of this paragraph, see Thomas W. Allen's Oxford edition of Homer, vol. V (1912), pp. 108-9.

6. William T. Avery, "Homeric Hospitality in Alcaeus and Horace," *Classical Philology*, LIX (1964), 107-9, makes an interesting attempt to demonstrate the influence of *Iliad* IX, lines 185 ff. on Alcaeus's Z 14.

7. Throughout this discussion of diction and style my major debts are to Edgar Lobel's monumental Introductions to his editions of Sappho (Oxford, 1925) and of Alcaeus (Oxford, 1927); the commentaries by Denys Page in his *Sappho and Alcaeus* (Oxford, 1955); A. E. Harvey, "Homeric Epithets in Greek Lyric Poetry," *The Classical Quarterly*, N. S. VII (1957), 206-23; Irena Kazik-Zawadzka, *De Sapphicae Alcaicaeque Elocutionis Colore Epico* (Wrocław, 1958); and R. J. Cunliffe, *A Lexicon of the Homeric Dialect* (Norman, Okla., 1963). Important also are Eva-Maria Hamm, *Grammatik zu Sappho und Alkaios* (Berlin, 1958); and Alessandra Romè, "L'Uso degli Epiteti in Saffo e Alceo con Riferimento alla Tradizione Epico-Rapsodica," *Studi Classici e Orientali*, XIV (1965), 210-46. Romè offers a list, with references, of all the epithets employed by Sappho and Alcaeus. Kazik-Zawadzka's very useful work is marred somewhat by an inability to appreciate the logical cogency of Lobel's methodology (see, e.g., her remarks on pp. 12-13).

8. For brief explanations of the Homeric formula see Lattimore (above, note 1), pp. 37-40 and Kirk (above, note 3), pp. 4-9.

9. In the case of each example only one Homeric occurrence will usually be cited, though in fact more, sometimes many more, may exist.

10. The prefix *za* (= *dia*) is certainly intensive. See Page (above, note 7), p. 266; Hamm (above, note 7), pp. 26 (paragraph 52 b) and 110 (paragraph 195 a); and Romè (above, note 7), p. 242.

11. For a rather full list of Alcaeus's debts to Homer in this broader usage see Kazik-Zawadzka (above, note 7), pp. 102-4.

12. See Page (above, note 7), p. 278 and, e.g., *Iliad* IX, line 637.

13. See *Iliad* XII, line 88; XIV, line 236; *Odyssey* IV, line 153; and VIII, line 86. I again remind my reader that the version of Q 1 here used is that by Lloyd-Jones (see above, note 5), not that of Lobel and Page's *Poetarum Lesbiorum Fragmenta*.

14. On the epic tone of lines 32-34 of G 2, see Harvey (above, note 7), p. 221; and Romè (above, note 7), pp. 236-38.

15. *Iliad* III, lines 336-37 (= XVI, lines 137-38). The translation is by Lattimore (above, note 1), p. 109.

16. The monumental and definitive discussion of this influence is in Lobel's Introductions (above, note 7). For statements of Lobel's conclusion, see his Sappho edition, pp. xxvii and lxxiv-lxxvi and his Alcaeus edition, pp. xi-xvii. Despite Lobel's hesitation (see his Alcaeus edition, p. ix and n. 2), I will follow Kazik-Zawadzka (above, note 7), pp. 15 and 97-98, regarding all non-Aeolic elements in Alcaeus's language as of epic origin.

17. On the words here discussed, see Lobel's edition of Sappho (above, note 7), pp. lxxiv-lxxv; Lobel's edition of Alcaeus (above, note 7), pp. xlv-xlvii; Page (above, note 7), pp. 226, 284, and 287; and Kazik-Zawadzka (above, note 7), pp. 27, 30-31, 34, 37, 48, 59, 60, 62-63, 71-72, and 98.

18. On the inflections here discussed, see Lobel's edition of Alcaeus (above, note 7), pp. xlviii-xlix; Page (above, note 7), pp. 276-77 and 313; and Kazik-Zawadzka (above, note 7), pp. 41-44, 47, and 97.

19. On the verb forms here discussed, see Lobel's edition of Sappho (above, note 7), pp. xl-xliii; Page (above, note 7), pp. 277 and 280; and Kazik-Zawadzka (above, note 7), pp. 51-52.

20. The translation is by Lattimore (above, note 1), p. 159.

21. For discussion cf basic metrical rules and Aeolic metrical schemes, the reader is referred to my last two chapters. On Alcaeus's use of epic correption and synizesis, see Lobel's edition of Alcaeus (above, note 7), pp. lx-lxii; Page (above, note 7), pp. 266 and 312; and Kazik-Zawadzka (above, note 7), pp. 20-22.

22. The final syllable of *beleos* should actually be scanned long because of its position at the end of a verse.

23. On these two hymns, see my chapter "Myth, Legend, and Hymn," and Page (above, note 2), pp. 268-72.

24. Scholarly opinion varies widely. E.g., A. R. Burn, *The World of Hesiod* (New York, 1966), p. 31 places Hesiod's lifetime "towards the end of the ninth century B.C.," while H. J. Rose, *A Handbook of Greek Literature* (New York, 1960), p. 65, chooses simply the eighth century.

25. On the dialect and meter in which Hesiod wrote see M. L. West, *Hesiod: Theogony* (Oxford, 1966), pp. 79-101. West's conclusions are summarized on p. 79 ("the dialect of Hesiod's poems

is ... essentially the same as that of Homer") and p. 91 ("the structure and characteristics of Hesiod's hexameters are in general identical with those of Homer's"). On the content of the *Works and Days* and the *Theogony*, see Rose (above, note 24), pp. 57-63.

26. This translation is in the Loeb edition (London and Cambridge, Mass., 1936), pp. 46-47. I have, however, replaced Evelyn-White's "grass-hopper" with "cicada."

27. The Greek text here translated by me is as arranged by Page (above, note 2), p. 303. Cf. the text offered by Carlo Gallavotti, *Saffo e Alceo*, vol. II (Naples, 1957), pp. 24-26.

28. For two other possible instances of Hesiodic influence on Alcaeus, see Page (above, note 2), pp. 255 and 273-74. Alcaeus may have borrowed from one of Hesiod's lost works in his Hymn to Hermes (item 308 in Lobel and Page), and there is a corrupt two-verse fragment (item 317 in Lobel and Page) that seems to be modeled on Hesiod's statement that Zeus gave Endymion permission to choose the time of his own death. The Hesiod reference to Endymion is Fr. 11 in A. Rzach's Teubner edition of Hesiod's *Carmina* (Leipzig, 1902), p. 134.

29. On Archilochus in general see especially C. M. Bowra, *Early Greek Elegists* (Cambridge, Mass., 1938), pp. 7-13; A. R. Burn, *The Lyric Age of Greece* (London, 1960), pp. 157-70; Rose (above, note 24), pp. 89-91; Hermann Fränkel, *Dichtung und Philosophie des fruhen Griechentums* (Munich, 1962), pp. 147-70; Albin Lesky, *A History of Greek Literature*, trans. James Willis and Cornelis de Heer (London, 1966), pp. 110-14; and Frederic Will, *Archilochos* (New York, 1969) in Twayne's World Authors Series.

30. The numbering of Archilochus's fragments is that of Ernst Diehl in his Teubner edition (*Anthologia Lyrica Graeca*, fasc. 3 [Leipzig, 1964]). All translations of Archilochus are by Richmond Lattimore, *Greek Lyrics* (Chicago and London, 1960), pp. 1-6.

31. The surviving text of Alcaeus's poem, together with the pertinent testimonia is listed as Z 105 in Lobel and Page's *Poetarum Lesbiorum Fragmenta* (Oxford, 1955), p. 287. On this poem see also Page (above, note 2), pp. 152-53; Gallavotti (above, note 27), p. 49; and Max Treu (ed. and tr.), *Alkaios* (Munich, 1963), pp. 88-89.

32. See the pertinent section of my chapter, "Similes and Metaphors."

33. On this identification, see Page (above, note 2), pp. 231-33.

34. *Allegories*, Ch. 5, 3-4. For Greek text of Heraclitus's comments, see Félix Buffière's Budé ed. (Paris, 1962) and Diehl (above, note 30), p. 25.

35. This translation is by Lattimore (above, note 30), pp. 42-43.

36. See, for example, Will (above, note 29), pp. 90-91.

37. See Fragment 76 of Archilochus in Diehl's *Anthologia Lyrica Graeca* (above, note 30) and C. M. Bowra, *Greek Lyric Poetry* (Oxford, 1961), p. 131.

38. Pseudo-Plutarch, *De Musica* 1132 D and 1133 C-D.

39. On Terpander, see especially *De Musica* 1132 C-1134 E *passim*, 1140 F, and 1146 B-C.

40. On Arion, see especially Herodotus I, 23-24 and A. W. Pickard-Cambridge, *Dithyramb, Tragedy and Comedy* (Oxford, 1962), pp. 11-13 and 97-101.

41. Bowra (above, note 37), p. 134. The Sapphic fragment is 102 in Lobel and Page's edition, and its translation is by Bowra, p. 134.

42. These verses are preserved by Plutarch, *Septem Sapientium Convivium* 157 D-E.

43. On the hidden meaning of the Eresos song, see A. v. Blumenthal, "Beobachtungen zu griechischen Texten II," *Hermes*, LXXV (1940), 125-27 and Bowra (above, note 37), pp. 131-32.

44. On this society see A. Andrewes, *The Greek Tyrants* (New York and Evanston, 1956), pp. 92-99 and Burn (above, note 29), pp. 226-46.

45. On these meters, see Chapters 9 and 10 of this book.

46. On the preservation of the poetry of Sappho and Alcaeus, see especially Lobel's edition of Sappho (Oxford, 1925), pp. ix-xiii; Carlo Gallavotti, *Saffo e Alceo*, vol. I (Naples, 1962), pp. 7-26; and Treu's survey in Pauly-Wissowa, Supplementband XI (1968), coll. 8-10. For Alcaeus, cf. Treu (above, note 31), pp. 128-30.

47. On Alcaeus's use of epic phraseology, see the first section of this chapter and the bibliography there cited. On Sappho's, especially Page (above, note 2), pp. 67-68 and the articles by Harvey (above, note 7), pp. 209-11 and 220 and by Romè (above, note 7).

48. On the substance of this paragraph, see the Introductions to Lobel's editions of Sappho and Alcaeus (above, note 7) and Page (above, note 7), pp. 65-67 and 327.

49. By far the longest and most important of these is Lobel and Page's Fragment 44, whose dialectal features are thoroughly and authoritatively analyzed by Page (above, note 7), pp. 63-70.

50. My interpretation of Z 61 is based primarily on W. Ferrari, "Due note su *hagnos*," *Studi Italiani di Filologia Classica*, XVII (1940), 38-53; Page (above, note 2), p. 108, n. 1; Bowra (above, note 37), pp. 238-39; and Treu (above, note 31), p. 180. For an interpretation that is more abstract and differs from mine in numerous ways, see Bruno Gentili, "La veneranda Saffo," *Quaderni Urbinati di Cultura Classica*, II (1966), 37-62.

51. The suggestion was made by Gallavotti (above, note 27), p. 39. Other editors who regard Z 61 as by Alcaeus are J. M. Edmonds in his Loeb edition (*Lyra Graeca*, vol. I [1922], pp. 398-99);

Théodore Reinach and Aimé Puech in the Budé edition of Sappho
and Alcaeus (1937), p. 116; and Treu (above, note 31), pp. 62-63
and 180.

52. Bowra (above, note 37), p. 239: "we cannot doubt that it
was written by Alcaeus, since there is nobody else whose words to
her would have survived."

53. So Ferrari (above, note 50), pp. 38-51, whose judgment on
this point is endorsed even by Gentili (above, note 50), p. 37.

54. This translation is by Page (above, note 2), p. 4.

55. Willis Barnstone (tr.), *Sappho* (Garden City, 1965), pp. 68-69.
I have rejected Barnstone's arrangement whereby Alcaeus's Z 61 is
treated as the first verse of this dialogue. The joining of these two
fragments has been favored by, e.g., Paul Maas, "Ährenlese," *Sokrates,*
VIII (1920), 20-25.

56. The Greek text of all the ancient comments pertinent to the
interpretation of the fragment is given by Page (above, note 2),
p. 104.

57. Page (above, note 2), p. 321.

58. Maas (above, note 55), pp. 21-23 and Page (above, note 2),
pp. 108-9.

59. With regard to the influence of Sapphic Fragment 137 on this
vase scene, I am neither so skeptical as Page (above, note 2), p. 108,
nor so all-believing as Ch. Picard, "Sur la Rencontre d'Alcée et de
Sappho," *Revue des Études Grecques,* LXI (1948), pp. 338-44.
Cf. Lesky (above, note 29), pp. 142-43. For photographs of the vase
scene, see Plate 64 in Furtwängler-Reichhold, vol. II and Wolfgang
Schadewaldt, *Sappho* (Potsdam, 1950), opposite p. 56.

Chapter Eight

1. On the loss of Alcaeus's poetry and its subsequent fortunes,
see especially Edgar Lobel's edition of Sappho (Oxford, 1925), pp.
ix-xxv; Théodore Reinach and Aimé Puech's Budé edition of Alcaeus
and Sappho (Paris, 1937), pp. 21-25; Gilbert Highet, *The Classical
Tradition* (New York and London, 1949), pp. 220-21; and Max
Treu's history of the Alcaeus papyrus finds in Pauly-Wissowa,
Supplementband XI (1968), coll. 8-10.

2. Horace through his *Odes* I, 14 was largely responsible for the
literary propagation of Alcaeus's Ship of Party allegory. For the
direct metrical and stylistic influence of Alcaeus on Tennyson, however, see Hallam Lord Tennyson's edition of his father's works, vol. I
(New York, 1908), pp. 765-66; W. Rhys Roberts, *Dionysius of
Halicarnassus: The Three Literary Letters* (Cambridge, 1901), pp.
x-xi; and my discussion of Tennyson's *Milton* in Ch. 9 of this book.

3. My major secondary debt in this section is to Reinach and

Puech (above, note 1), pp. 15-20. See pp. 15-16 for my following remarks about Dicaearchus, Aristophanes of Byzantium, and Aristarchus.

4. On this canon see C. M. Bowra, *Greek Lyric Poetry* (Oxford, 1961), p. 2.

5. On the form in which the essay *On Imitation* has survived, see Roberts (above, note 2), pp. 27-28; S. F. Bonner, *The Literary Treatises of Dionysius of Halicarnassus* (Cambridge, 1939), pp. 39-40; and G. M. A. Grube, *The Greek and Roman Critics* (Toronto, 1965), pp. 209-11. The text I have used is that by H. Usener, *Librorum de Imitatione Reliquiae* (Bonn, 1889), pp. 19-20 (II, 1-8 of *De Imitatione*).

6. On this essay, see Roberts (above, note 2), pp. 8-19 (esp. 18-19); Bonner (above, note 5), pp. 71-78; and Grube (above, note 5), pp. 217-25.

7. A recent and readable study of Quintilian is that by George Kennedy, *Quintilian* (New York, 1969), in Twayne's World Authors Series.

8. On Alcaeus's references to youths and women, see Denys Page, *Sappho and Alcaeus* (Oxford, 1955), pp. 294-99.

9. These Horace translations are by James Michie, *The Odes of Horace* (New York, 1963), pp. 63-65.

10. I regard M 10 (b) and P 2 (b), both discussed by Page (above, note 8) on pp. 296-98, as fragmented beyond even a speculative explanation of their content.

11. A Dinnomenes is also mentioned in Z 60.

12. Melanippus appears in B 6 and Z 105, and Bycchis in Z 11, D 15 (cf. X 16), X 3, and a scholion to D 2.

13. On Demetrius, see Roberts, *Demetrius on Style* (Cambridge, 1902) and Grube (above, note 5), pp. 110-21.

14. This is fragment 223 in F. W. Hall and W. M. Geldart's Oxford text of Aristophanes (1906-7).

15. For full discussion of Aristotle's citation, see the section on Sappho and Alcaeus in Chapter 7 of this book.

16. The following translation is by W. C. Helmbold in the Loeb edition of Plutarch's *Moralia*, vol. IX (1961), p. 395. For clarity's sake, however, I have retained the Greek name "Eros," which Helmbold translates as "Love."

17. The Alcaean citation in Plutarch's *Obsolescence of Oracles* (410 C) is also introduced for analogical, literary adornment. Cf. that in *On Love of Wealth* (525 A-B).

18. The Aristides passages in question are at I, 821; II, 273; and II, 155. For a convenient text and translation of Aristides's citations, see J. M. Edmonds, *Lyra Graeca*, vol. I (London and New York, 1922), pp. 338-41 and 360-61.

19. Following is a full list of the passages in which Athenaeus's Alcaeus citations appear. In each instance the number in parentheses gives the pages on which the Athenaeus passage is quoted in Greek and then translated into English by Edmonds (above, note 18), vol. I. I, 22 f (420-21); II, 38 e (424-25); III, 73 e (412-13); III, 85 f (376-77); VII, 311 a (360-61); X, 425 c (324-25); X, 430 a-c (348-49, 416-17, 420-21, 422-23); XI, 460 d (358-59); XI, 478 b (428-29); XI, 481 a (424-25); XIV, 627 a (332-33); XV, 674 c (416-17).

20. Himerius's summary occurs in *Oration* XIV, 10-11. On this summary, see Page (above, note 8), pp. 244-46.

21. This is the Loeb translation by W. C. Wright, *The Works of the Emperor Julian*, vol. II (1949), p. 421.

22. The Libanius passage (*Oration* XIII, 5) is quoted by Page (ed.), *Lyrica Graeca Selecta* (Oxford, 1968), p. 88.

23. On Heraclitus and pertinent bibliography, see above Ch. 4, section II with notes 14 and 16.

24. For Hephaestion's citations of Alcaeus, see Edmonds (above, note 18), vol. I, pp. 318-21, 330-31, 350-51, 354-57, 374-79, 398-99, 402-5.

25. Page (above, note 8), pp. 152-53.

26. This translation is by Aubrey de Selincourt, *Herodotus: The Histories* (Penguin Books, 1954), p. 349.

27. I, however, see no reason for regarding the reference to Alcaeus as a marginal note that has gotten into Strabo's text, as does H. L. Jones in his Loeb edition of *The Geography of Strabo*, vol. VI (1929), p. 76, n. 1 and p. 77, n. 2.

28. This translation is by Jones (above, note 27), vol. IV (1927), p. 329.

29. My major debt in this section is to Eduard Fraenkel, *Horace* (Oxford, 1957), pp. 154-78. I am also indebted in varying degrees to the books and commentaries listed above in Ch. 4, n. 12.

30. On Horace's adaptation of Aeolic meters, see, e.g., L. P. Wilkinson, *Horace and His Lyric Poetry* (Cambridge, 1968), pp. 10-13 and 143-45.

31. These translations from *Epistle* I, 19 are by S. P. Bovie, *The Satires and Epistles of Horace* (Chicago, 1959), p. 221.

32. All renderings of Horace's Odes in this section are taken from the excellent translation of the Odes by James Michie (above, note 9).

33. Wilkinson (above, note 30), p. 60. The Greek poems in question are Archilochus, 6 (Diehl) and Alcaeus, Z 105 (Lobel and Page). Lobel and Page give the pertinent Herodotus and Strabo passages.

34. For my interpretation of the third stanza of *Odes* I, 10, see

Page (above, note 8), pp. 252-57 and Fraenkel (above, note 29), pp. 161-66.

35. On the relation between these two poems, see Page (above, note 8), p. 324 (item VI) and Fraenkel (above, note 29), p. 178.

36. Quintilian, *Institutio Oratoria* VIII, 6, 44. On Alcaeus's nautical allegories, see above Chapter 4, section II.

37. The Alcaeus translation is by Willis Barnstone, *Greek Lyric Poetry* (Bantam Classics, 1967), p. 55. Here, as elsewhere in this section, the translation of the Horatian Ode is by Michie (above, note 9).

Chapter Nine

1. Good, readable introductions to English versification, including metrics, are provided by George B. Woods, *Versification in English Poetry* (Chicago, 1958) and Karl Shapiro and Robert Beum, *A Prosody Handbook* (New York, 1965). An excellent book that ranges more widely is X. J. Kennedy, *An Introduction to Poetry* (Boston and Toronto, 1966).

2. This statement, of course, excludes experiments in quantitative metrics, such as those discussed by Shapiro and Beum (above, note 1), pp. 153-58. An experiment of this type by Tennyson will soon be discussed in detail.

3. William W. Goodwin and Charles B. Gulick, *Greek Grammar* (Boston, 1930), p. 344, compare the meter of a modern Greek translation of the first two verses of the *Odyssey* with that of their original. See also Paul Maas, *Greek Metre*, trans. Hugh Lloyd-Jones (Oxford, 1962), pp. 1-22.

4. Most of the suggested pronunciations and illustrative English words in this and the following vowel and diphthong tables are taken from Henry L. Crosby and John N. Shaeffer, *An Introduction to Greek* (Boston, 1928), pp. xxii-xxv. In the case of *upsilon* (both long and short), however, I have catered to my English speaking readers. It goes without saying that these suggested pronunciations are in general only the best approximations we can arrive at and that no one can reproduce *precisely* the phonemes of ancient Greek. The definitive work on the subject is now W. B. Stanford, *The Sound of Greek* (Berkeley and Los Angeles, 1967).

5. The traditional transliteration of *upsilon* (both long and short) is *y*, as in the proper name *Dionysus*, the prefixes *hypo* and *hyper*, and in such words as *psychiatrist* and *physics*. Upsilon, however, sometimes appears as *u* in whole words that are transliterated directly into English from Greek without an intermediate stage in Latin: e.g., *kudos* and *hubris* (which also appears as *hybris*).

6. A more precise term than "verse" would be "period." To

simplify my explanatory vocabulary, however, I have avoided "period" both here and elsewhere, and will use instead "line" or "verse." For the "period" and its features see Bruno Snell, *Griechische Metrik*, 3rd ed. (Göttingen, 1962), pp. 4-5; and James W. Halporn, Martin Ostwald, and Thomas G. Rosenmeyer, *The Meters of Greek and Latin Poetry* (Indianapolis, 1963), pp. 6-8. (This last work will hereafter be cited as Rosenmeyer, who was responsible for its Greek portion.)

7. In distinguishing between *anceps* and *brevis in longo* I follow Snell (above, note 6), p. 4, n. 3; Rosenmeyer (above, note 6), pp. 7 and 10; and Maas (above, note 3), p. 29 (paragraph 34). Cf. the obscure query by A. M. Dale in her review of the first edition of Snell's *Griechische Metrik* in *Gnomon*, XXVIII (1956), 193.

8. But see Stanford (above, note 4), pp. 83-84, who recognizes a limited awareness of rhyme among Greek poets.

9. On stress, quantity, and color see Shapiro and Beum (above, note 1), pp. 8-25 and Stanford (above, note 4), pp. 39-43.

10. The poem under consideration is the first Alcaeus selection in Lattimore's *Greek Lyrics* (Chicago, 1960), pp. 42-43. That this is a stress rather than a quantitative adaptation like Tennyson's *Milton* (to be examined presently) is clear from the large number of syllables that would violate the law of length by position if Lattimore were attempting to employ quantitative metrics: e.g., the metrical scheme of the Alcaic stanza would dictate the scansion of

$$\_ \; \cup \; \cup \; \_$$

"Now from this side" (stanza 1, verse 2); yet both "from" and "this" should be scanned as long by position, since the vowel in each is followed by two consonants. Also, if my memory serves me correctly, Lattimore *seemed* to indicate in a brief, informal conversation with me at the Fourth International Congress of Classical Studies (held in Philadelphia in August, 1964) that his translations of Sappho and Alcaeus in *Greek Lyrics* were stress adaptations of the quantitative originals.

11. On the pitch accent of ancient Greek and its gradual change to a stress accent in modern Greek see Goodwin and Gulick (above, note 3), p. 28 (paragraph 127); Herbert W. Smyth, *Greek Grammar*, revised by Gordon M. Messing (Cambridge, Mass., 1956), p. 37 (paragraph 151); and Stanford (above, note 4), pp. 30-33, 59-60, 63, 146-48, and (for a summary) 157-60.

12. This is the system of recitation urged by Stanford (above, note 4), whose whole book is an advocacy of a return to ancient manners of pronunciation. See esp. pp. 1-7 and 122-39. For an opposing point of view see Maas (above, note 3), pp. 55-58.

13. A few metricians have refused to abandon the theory that the ancient Greeks recited poetry with an *ictus* (in the sense of a

"stress"); and the *ictus* is presented as virtually fact in Goodwin and Gulick's much used grammar (above, note 3), pp. 344 and 346 (paragraphs 1626, 1631, and 1632). A. M. Dale, "Greek Metric 1936-1957," *Lustrum*, II (1957), 20, however, correctly observes: "Certainly there should be no *theory* of 'ictus' in the sense of purely metrical stresses, since there is no evidence whatever for its existence in Greek."

14. *The Works of Alfred Lord Tennyson*, annotated by Alfred Lord Tennyson and edited by Hallam Lord Tennyson, vol. I (New York, 1908), pp. 616 and 765-66.

15. The signal success of Kennedy's introduction to the study of poetry (above, note 1) is due in large measure to his including, except in rare instances, only poems that are short enough to be quoted in full. In selecting for illustrative purposes Housman's "With rue my heart is laden" and Tennyson's *Milton* and in quoting all of each poem, I follow Kennedy's judicious practice.

16. On this point see, e.g., Denys Page, *Sappho and Alcaeus* (Oxford, 1955), p. 328 (item ix); Maas (above, note 3), p. 76; and Rosenmeyer (above, note 6), pp. 5 and 34.

Chapter Ten

1. On the metrical theories of the ancients see Ulrich von Wilamowitz-Moellendorff, *Griechische Verskunst* (Berlin, 1921), pp. 58-85; Bruno Snell, *Griechische Metrik*, 3rd ed. (Göttingen, 1962), p. 54; and Paul Maas, *Greek Metre*, trans. Hugh Lloyd-Jones (Oxford, 1962), p. 5.

2. For this distinction between "Aeolic" and "non-Aeolic" meters see my observations at the end of this chapter. My statistics here and elsewhere in this chapter are compiled from the metrical conspectus by Denys Page, *Sappho and Alcaeus* (Oxford, 1955), pp. 323-26.

3. Page (above, note 2), pp. 318-29 ("Appendix on Metres"); and James W. Halporn, Martin Ostwald, and Thomas G. Rosenmeyer, *The Meters of Greek and Latin Poetry* (Indianapolis, 1963), pp. 29-34. This second work is cited as Rosenmeyer, since he is responsible for its entire Greek section.

4. E.g., by William E. McCulloh, who prepared the "Metrical Tables and Metrical Index" to Willis Barnstone's Sappho translations (Garden City, 1965), pp. 187-96. McCulloh without comment recommends simultaneously as introductory reading both *The Meters of Greek and Latin Poetry* and Page's "Appendix on Metres." Also, McCulloh's tables reflect some confusing attempts at a synthesis.

5. A. M. Dale, "The Metrical Units of Greek Lyric Verse," *Classical Quarterly*, XLIV (1950), 138-48 (esp. 142-43); XLV

(1951), 20-30 (esp. 21) and 119-29 (esp. 124-28). Bruno Snell (above, note 1), pp. 34-38.

6. On the "period" see Snell (above, note 1), pp. 4-5; and Rosenmeyer (above, note 3), pp. 6-8.

7. I follow Snell (above, note 1), p. 36 (the entry for A 54) in treating this form as a single verse composed of two glyconics and an iambic metron. It should not be diagrammed as a two verse stanza because of word overlap between the two glyconic units at Z 34, line 4 (*an-drōn*) and in both lines of Z 37 (*Aristodā-mon* and *penich-ros*). If the form is regarded as *gl+*, *Λgl, ia* (that is, if with *Papyrus Oxyrhynchus*, xxi, 2295 and 2296 the division is made after the ninth rather than the eighth syllable), the three instances of word overlap just mentioned are avoided; but three new instances are introduced into Z 34. In other words, no reasonable division of the form into a two verse stanza can eliminate word overlap between verses.

8. Despite the fragmentary condition of A 5 and D 9 (the only two poems in which Alcaeus uses this particular stanza form), Page (above, note 2) confidently recognizes the form in his "Appendix on Metres" (see p. 324). Horace employs this stanza form in nine Odes (I. 6, 15, 24, 33; II. 12; III. 10, 16; IV. 5, 12), and Page must have utilized these Odes in reconstructing it for Alcaeus.

9. Page (above, note 2), p. 318.

10. See above, note 7 for my reasons for treating this metrical pattern as a single verse rather than as a two verse stanza form.

11. See above, note 8 for the problems connected with reconstructing this stanza form.

12. This distinction between the "Aeolic" and the "non-Aeolic" among Alcaeus's and Sappho's lyric meters is implicit throughout Snell's discussion of "The Aeolic Poets" (above, note 1), pp. 34-38 and is often hinted at (e.g., p. 36, n. 1). Rosenmeyer (above, note 3), pp. 29-34 makes the distinction more explicit by entitling his comparable section "Aeolic Meters" instead of "The Aeolic Poets" and by introducing such statements as "the glyconic is the basic Aeolic meter" (p. 30).

Selected Bibliography

PRIMARY SOURCES
(Texts, translations, and commentaries)

BARNSTONE, WILLIS. *Greek Lyric Poetry.* New York and Toronto: Bantam Books, 2nd ed., 1967. Contains translations of twenty-six Alcaean fragments. The translations are free and succeed as English poetry, but are often based on imaginary or reconstructed Greek texts.

DIEHL, ERNST. *Anthologia Lyrica Graeca.* I (including Alcaeus), Leipzig: Teubner, 2nd ed., 1935. Greek text with substantial apparatus and thorough presentation of the testimonia. Antiquated only because of the continuing publication of papyrus fragments.

EDMONDS, J. M. *Lyra Graeca* (Loeb ed.). I (including Alcaeus), London: William Heinemann and New York: G. P. Putnam's Sons, 1922. Greek text with facing English translation. Now antiquated because of the continuing publication of papyrus fragments of Alcaeus's poetry; but very useful for furnishing a full text, with translation, of passages in which Alcaeus is quoted or summarized by ancient writers.

LATTIMORE, RICHMOND. *Greek Lyrics.* Chicago: The University of Chicago Press, 2nd ed., 1960. Contains translations of seven of the longer Alcaean fragments. The translations are straightforward and reflect the actual condition of the Greek text.

LLOYD-JONES, HUGH. "The Cologne Fragment of Alcaeus," *Greek, Roman and Byzantine Studies,* IX (1968), 125-39. The most recent and the definitive edition of Q 1, whose version in Lobel and Page's *Poetarum Lesbiorum Fragmenta* (see below) has been antiquated by a new papyrus find.

LOBEL, EDGAR. *Sapphous Melē: The Fragments of the Lyrical Poems of Sappho.* Oxford: The Clarendon Press, 1925.

————. *Alkaiou Melē: The Fragments of the Lyrical Poems of Alcaeus.* Oxford: The Clarendon Press, 1927. This and the preceding edition, though their Greek texts have been superseded by those of later editions, offer Introductions that are masterful and definitive studies of the language of Alcaeus and Sappho.

LOBEL, EDGAR, and DENYS PAGE. *Poetarum Lesbiorum Fragmenta.* Oxford: The Clarendon Press, 1955. At present the definitive edition of Alcaeus and Sappho.

181

ALCAEUS

182

[THE] OXYRHYNCHUS PAPYRI. London: The Egypt Exploration Society. Vols. XXIII (ed. Lobel, 1956), XXIX (ed. Page, 1963), and XXXV (ed. Lobel, 1968) contain Alcaeus material not available for Lobel and Page's major ed. (see above).

PAGE, DENYS. *Sappho and Alcaeus.* Oxford: The Clarendon Press, 1955. Text and translation of all the longer and many of the shorter poems, together with commentaries and discussions of Sappho's and Alcaeus's poetry. Indispensable to the study of Alcaeus.

————. *Lyrica Graeca Selecta* (an Oxford Classical Text). Oxford: The Clarendon Press, 1968. A fine edition, which contains the Greek text of all but the most mutilated Alcaean fragments.

REINACH, THÉODORE and AIMÉ PUECH. *Alcée. Sappho* (Budé ed.). Paris: Société d'Édition "Les Belles Lettres," 1937. Greek text with facing French translation. Text now antiquated, but good Introduction to Alcaeus.

SECONDARY SOURCES

ANDREWES, A. *The Greek Tyrants.* First published, 1956; reprinted as a Harper Torchbook, New York and Evanston: Harper and Row, 1963. Ch. VIII ("Aristocratic Disorder at Mytilene") provides a sound, readable introduction to Mytilenean politics during the period of Alcaeus.

BOWRA, C. M. *Greek Lyric Poetry.* Oxford: The Clarendon Press, 2nd ed., 1961. A classic introduction to Greek lyric (but "lyric" treated in the narrow sense of the word). Separate chapters on Alcaeus and on Sappho.

BURN, A. R. *The Lyric Age of Greece.* London: Edward Arnold, 1960. Beautifully written and highly perceptive. Fine chapter on "The Lyric Age of Lesbos."

COOK, J. M. *Greek Settlement in the Eastern Aegean and Asia Minor.* Cambridge: Cambridge University Press, 1961. Contains a history of the Aeolic settlement of Lesbos. To be published eventually as a chapter in vol. II of the revised *Cambridge Ancient History.*

DALE, A. M. "The Metrical Units of Greek Lyric Verse," *The Classical Quarterly,* XLIV (1950), 138-48; XLV (1951), 20-30 and 119-219. Contains a treatment of Aeolic meters adopted by Page in his *Sappho and Alcaeus* and alternative to that presented by Snell and Rosenmeyer (see under Primary Sources the entry Page, and under Secondary Sources the entries Snell and Halporn).

FRAENKEL, EDUARD. *Horace.* Oxford: The Clarendon Press, 1957. Section titled "Odes related to Alcaeus" is basic to the study of Alcaeus's literary influence.

HALPORN, JAMES W., MARTIN OSTWALD, and THOMAS G. ROSEN-
MEYER. *The Meters of Greek and Latin Poetry* (in The Library
of Liberal Arts). Indianapolis and New York: The Bobbs-
Merrill Co., 1963. The section on the "Aeolic Meters" is by
Rosenmeyer, who adapts Snell's treatment of these same meters
(see below under Snell).

HARVEY, A. E. "Homeric Epithets in Greek Lyric Poetry," *The
Classical Quarterly*, LI (1957), 206-33. Good, stimulating literary criticism. Treats Sappho and Alcaeus prominently.

LESKY, ALBIN. *A History of Greek Literature*. Translated by James
Willis and Cornelis de Heer. London: Methuen, 1966. Per-
ceptive and reliable. Contains a special section on "The Lesbian
Lyric."

PAGE, DENYS. *Sappho and Alcaeus*. See Page, under Primary Sources.

SNELL, BRUNO. *Griechische Metrik*. Göttingen: Vandenhoeck and
Ruprecht, 3rd ed., 1962. Contains a sensitive and incisive
analysis of the meters used by Sappho and Alcaeus.

TREU, MAX. *Paulys Realenzyklopädie der classischen Altertums-
wissenschaft*, Supplementband XI (Stuttgart: Alfred Drucken-
müller, 1968), coll. 8-19. A supplement to Crusius's 1893
Alcaeus article. Valuable for bibliographical data and for its
history of Alcaean papyrus finds.

WILKINSON, L. P. *Horace and His Lyric Poetry*. Cambridge: Cam-
bridge University Press, 2nd ed., 1951; first paperback ed., 1968.
Contains, *passim*, perceptive discussions of Horace's debt to
Alcaeus.

Index

185

METRICAL TERMS

GREEK WORDS

ALCAEAN CORPUS
(after Lobel-Page; see Preface)

DATE DUE